THE CITIZEN'S GUIDE TO RESEARCH

by Ashley Warren

THE CITIZEN'S GUIDE TO RESEARCH

A Practical Guide to Understanding Research
in the Era of Big Data

To Andrew

TABLE OF CONTENTS

INTRODUCTION

Welcome to the Citizen's Guide to Research!

It is my hope that this book will become a staple in your personal library. It's split into two parts: how research is conducted, and how you can conduct your own research. As my graduate school professors insisted, research is best learned when you can actually get out there and try your hand at it. There are also resources at the end that you can reference often.

This book originated as a weekly email series, and I'm heartened to see increased public interest in research. It's never been more important to be able to know how to evaluate credible sources, to understand basic statistics, and to have some insight into the research process.

Consider this your call to research, no matter your background, skills, or interests. Research is all around us, and we're better for it when we have the power to make data-driven choices about our own lives.

Happy researching!

Ashley Warren

PART 1

A PRIMER TO RESEARCH

CHAPTER 1
EAT ALL THE PASTA YOU WANT

Did you know that PASTA makes you SKINNY? I mean, science PROVED it! Look, I read about it:

SCIENCE JUST PROVED PASTA MAKES YOU SKINNY SO WE'RE GOING ON AN ALL-CARB DIET

That's a headline from a real publication. Sure, that particular site likes to have a sense of humor, but at the end of the day, it's not a satire site, so we can assume it's trying to be informative.

Could that headline sound any better to an Italian-American girl like me? I was intrigued, so I clicked, looking for the science to back up an excuse to gorge on tasty pasta (not that I ever need an excuse).

Wait a sec. The actual study isn't linked to in the article.

Instead, it links to another article in web publication Mic, titled "This Study on How Pasta Can Help You Lose Weight is Easily the Best Science of 2016." Aside from that dubious claim (I can appreciate the humor, but the best science of 2016 was arguably developments in space exploration and health... #buzzkill), the Mic article also links to *another* non-scientific article in the Telegraph.UK before it links to the actual study.

Luckily, the actual study is accessible for free, which isn't always the case with academic research.* The study *does* show a link between healthy weight maintenance and pasta consumption — in conjunction with an existing Mediterranean diet of fresh, seasonal produce, and locally-sourced fish.

So the headline is not necessarily false, but it's not necessarily true, either.

Hmm... anyone else in the mood for pasta primavera?

My anecdote is to help illustrate that science and research is all around us, and we consume it without realizing it. This, in many ways, is wonderful. However, there's a trend of what I think of as "headline science," where complex research is condensed into one clickbaity sentence. Unfortunately, these headline claims are actually false, or they just share one tiny part of the findings without the context.

And instead of going to the actual data — often locked behind a paywall, which we'll discuss in the coming chapters — journalists report on *other* journalist's articles. Remember the game, Telephone, where one person whispers a message into another's ear, and it gets passed around in a circle? By the end of the circle, the message has usually warped into something completely different. That's how headline science can work. Not only does it mislead readers and consumers, but it incorrectly shares researcher's findings, which can make an impact on their entire research discipline.

This isn't to disparage journalists. I used to be one — usually covering science! — so I totally get it. Being a journalist is hard, and they see a lot of news and science on a daily basis. All of us can chip in to be more critical readers.

Real research (especially in the health industry, which lends itself so well to clickbait) is complicated, highly technical, and very specific. It's rare that scientists and academics make claims that can be shared in a simplified way. A good scientist *should* be able to explain their research without jargon, but their actual process tends to be too technical for the "average" reader.

But you're not the average reader, are you?

* *"Association of pasta consumption with body mass index and waist-to-hip ratio: results from Moli-sani and INHES studies," accessible here: http://www.nature.com/ nutd/journal/v6/n7/full/nutd201620a.html?foxtrotcallback=true*

LESSON ACTIVITY

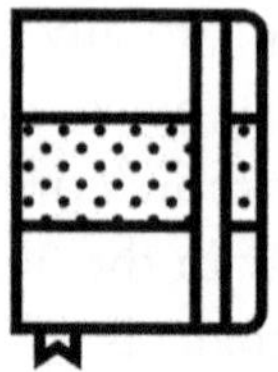

PART 1:

Grab a journal or a notetaking app, and make a note of anytime you come across an article, online or in print, that says something like:

"A study proved…"
"Scientists say/science says…"
"A report found…"

PART 2:

If you see a claim like that, see if the article links to any original data. If so, is the source a reliable source?

(It's OK if you don't know the answers to these questions yet. We'll cover them soon.)

CHAPTER 2
CREDIBILITY, SHMEDIBILITY

When I was teaching English 101, my students had to write a research paper on the topic of their choosing. As part of this assignment, they had to have a minimum of ten "reliable and credible sources." There was *immediate panic*. Does the local newspaper count as a "credible" source? Does an article in a medical journal? Does a blog? What's the difference, and how will I know if a source fits the criteria?

But after the research project was complete, one of my students came up to me and said: "I feel like I'll never be able to read anything ever again without questioning where the information came from."

Success! Welcome to the wonderful, frustrating, but ultimately satisfying, world of research.

Last chapter, we talked about looking for the source in an article that claims science "proved" something. But what happens next once you've found a source? How can you tell if the research has been credibly produced?

Let's talk specifically about published research articles found in research journals. This refers to the actual source of the data, where the researcher(s) share:

- An overview of their study, called the abstract;
- The purpose of the study and their research questions;
- A review of existing research on the topic, called the literature review;
- The steps and process of the study, called the methods;
- The findings of the study, called the results;
- A discussion about the findings and further implications of research;
- and the references cited throughout.

In chapter 1, we found a research article referenced in a Mic article about the weight-loss potential of pasta (which is linked to at the end of the chapter).

Here are three basic questions you can ask yourself when you find a research article to help evaluate its credibility:

QUESTION #1: WHERE IS THE RESEARCH PUBLISHED?

The first step is to see where the research article was published. Not all journals have the word "journal," in the title, but many do. See what you can find from the journal's main website. Is it connected to a university or research institute? Is it an industry publication? Is it an open access journal? (Hint: if you don't know what that means, you'll find out next chapter!)

QUESTION #2: IS THE JOURNAL "PEER-REVIEWED" OR "REFEREED"?

Peer-review means that other researchers in that field have reviewed a research article before it was published in the journal. This ensures that the process and findings make sense, and the researchers followed the scientific method and proper research ethics. Refereeing research like helps to hold researchers accountable for their results and their methodology.

If you're a student or community member with access to a library, an easy way to see if a journal or publication is peer-reviewed is to use a website called Ulrichsweb.com. You can search for a journal title, and it will tell you if that journal is refereed. If you don't have access to that website, you can look in the journal itself, or on the journal's website. (Or, ask a librarian! A good tip for most things in life.)

Keep in mind that not every single article in a peer-reviewed journal may have actually been peer-reviewed; sometimes journals publish book reviews or opinions that don't require a committee review process.

QUESTION #3: WHO CONDUCTED THE RESEARCH?

The names of the authors should be easily accessible, even if the article itself isn't. Can you find out where the authors are affiliated (for instance, their university of employment)? If there isn't any author data, what else can you find out about the researchers behind the study?

OPTIONAL QUESTION: IS THE RAW DATA AVAILABLE?

This isn't a deal-breaker, but for many researchers, being able to see the original data (such as the notes from a group study, spreadsheets with numbers, etc.) helps when determining accuracy and replicability in the findings. **Replicability** means that other researchers in the field could follow the same research process as outlined in the article to see if they receive similar results.

I want to clarify one thing: if you find articles that aren't in peer-reviewed, academic journals, it's OK! It doesn't mean that information doesn't matter or that it isn't good research. However, you will want to take into account potential biases or problems with the research methodology that haven't been addressed by the greater research community.

LESSON ACTIVITY

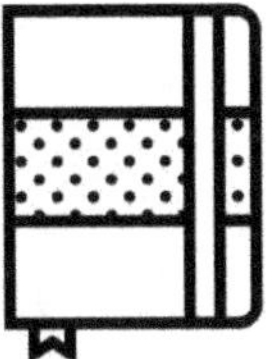

PART 1:

Now that you have some guidelines for what constitutes a "credible" research article, we're going to repeat chapter one's activity.

Find an article in a magazine or newspaper that references a "study," and see if the article links to the actual study.

PART 2:

Using the three questions above, see what you can find out to determine if the study is "credible."

CHAPTER 3
OPEN THE POD BAY DOORS

Read this in what you imagine to be my "stern teacher voice": Have you been doing your homework from chapters 1 and 2?

If not, here's the simple version: When you encounter a reference to a "study" — for example, in a magazine article about the health benefits of wheatgrass — see if you are able to track down the original study.

Easy, right? Yeah, not exactly.

Last chapter covered the basics of determining a study's credibility: meaning, what makes a researcher's findings, published in a research journal, reliable and scientific? Tracking a claim back to its original source, and evaluating the credibility of the results, is a great place to start. But what if you can't even access the original research?

For the purposes of this guide, we're talking specifically about research published in research journals. As you'll learn in the coming chapters, research and data takes many forms, and research articles in journals are just one form. But studies published as research articles still make up the bulk of how research is conducted, shared, funded, and used for impact in various industries (such as policy, education, or health).

And unless you are an academic, librarian, or high-level industry researcher, you're likely not being exposed to many research articles. Even journalists who report on the study findings are usually not accessing full articles.

That's because accessing research as a non-researcher (or as a citizen researcher, like you!) can be difficult and expensive. The vast majority of world-changing research is not accessible to the general public. Much of it is locked behind a paywall, costing anywhere from $10 to $100 to access a PDF of a study.

As citizen researchers, you *do* have options. (And no shortage of research memes:)

GO TO THE LIBRARY

This may seem obvious, but I can't tell you how often I see people ask where to find a research article. Most libraries pay for database access, and all you need is a library card. Depending on what article you're looking for, you may want to visit your local college or university library. University libraries have the most extensive access to research databases.

If you're not an alumni or affiliated with a university, you may need to pay a small fee to access anything at the library. This is to help cover their costs of paying for database access. But, in my opinion, a one-time fee of $20 is worth it for almost unlimited access to research and media.

READ OPEN ACCESS

The open access movement refers to research that is made public and freely available. The internet has made this a much more viable option for publishing and sharing research. PLOS (the Public Library of Science, a nonprofit) explains this well:

> *Most publishers own the rights to the articles in their journals. Anyone who wants to read the articles must pay to access them. Anyone who wants to use the articles in any way must obtain permission from the publisher and is often required to pay an additional fee.*
>
> *Although many researchers can access the journals they need via their institution and think that access is free, in reality it is not. The institution has often been involved in lengthy negotiations around the price of their site license and reuse of this content is limited.*
>
> *Paying for access to journals makes sense in the world of print publishing, where providing articles to each reader requires the production of physical copies of articles, but in the online world, with distribution as wide as the internet's reach, it makes much less sense.*

Open access journals are very similar to traditional journals and databases. In fact, many longtime databases now have open access options. The stigma of open access being less credible than traditionally published research is quickly changing as more and more researchers choose open access.

LESSON ACTIVITY

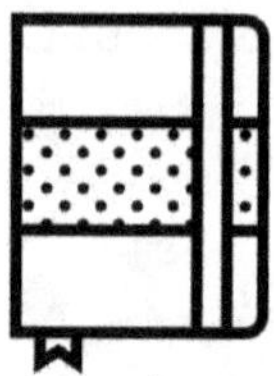

PART 1:

Find an open access journal using one of these links:

PLOS (plos.org)
Directory of Open Access Journals (doaj.org)

Look up a topic that interests you. See what articles you can find about that topic. Is there anything in the articles you find that you don't understand? Are you confused about any of the terminology you see? Write down anything you're not sure about.

PART 2:

Make it a goal to visit your local library once a month. You'll likely be surprised by all of the great resources a library has to offer, beyond books — movies, e-books/audiobooks, popular magazines, community events, and sometimes even tools or free food.

CHAPTER 4
YOU CAN (STUDY) DANCE IF YOU WANT TO

I once saw an article by Lifehacker in my newsfeed: "Scientists discover the ideal dance moves for women."

The headline caught my intention: "Scientists discover..." (Remember what we discussed in Chapter 1?) Before I proceeded to check out the article, I was struck by the comment section, particularly this exchange:

Commenter 1: I am so grateful this man wrote an article relaying information on how I should dance. I wonder who they believe women dance for? Like, ideal for whom?

Commenter 2: After reading that article, I HAD to read the publication because the article made it sound horrible. The person [who] wrote that for Lifehacker totally twisted the reason for the original research!

Commenter 1: Goodness, you are SO RIGHT. I went back and read the study, and how did the author of this article go from, "This is how women dance" to "This is ideally how women should dance"?

The gist is that a woman shared this article with her friend, and both were skeptical about the reporting of the article. So, they both went to look at the original research article. As you can see, one of the women commented, "The person [who] wrote that for Lifehacker totally twisted the reason for the original research!"

Major kudos to both of them for doing their homework! They weren't satisfied with just the reporting by the Lifehacker writer, so they followed the source of the research.

I continued to peruse the comments, many of which asked the same questions:

- What is the point of this research?
- Who *cares* what ideal dancing is?
- Why spend energy and funding on research like this when scientists can be solving cancer/climate change/etc.?

This kind of commentary happens a lot to researchers. It's important to clarify that not all scientists study the same science. That may seem obvious, but it's hard for people who aren't in the professional research world to know *who* does *what*.

The article referenced in the Lifehacker piece is open access, and tagged in *Scientific Reports* as "human behavior" and "social behavior." The lead researcher is Kristofer McCarty, from the Department of Psychology from Northumbria University. McCarty's area of research likely doesn't overlap with cancer research; from his other cited work, we can derive that his areas of research include behavior science, sexuality, and movement. Should we expect researchers like McCarty to answer all of the world's most pressing questions?

Which leads us to ask:

Is all research created equal?

There's no definitive way to answer this question. Research is a diverse world with new disciplines emerging all the time. Researchers aren't educated and trained to study every single scientific topic; that would be ineffective and virtually impossible. Typically, researchers like McCarty receive advanced degrees in a very, very specific area.

Instead, it's worth asking: what makes researchers come up with research topics? These are some of the main reasons:

Industry demand and funding.
The need to fund research can sometimes drive the topics that are researched. This doesn't have to be a bad thing; providing researchers with resources to run studies can help improve research processes and work toward breakthroughs faster. But it can prioritize some topics over others if industries intend to use particular findings for new products or developments.

Unexplored territory.
Since researchers are experts in their fields, they know what has been researched and what still needs to be explored. Many researchers are inspired or motivated by the work of their predecessors, and base new studies off of existing questions.

Curiosity — and potential long-term impact.
Even with expertise and a solid hypothesis in hand, researchers often can't predict what impact their findings may have.

For example, a study about female dance movements may lead to another study about the female cardiovascular system, which could lead to a new understanding of how to treat or identify diseases unique to this system... and so on. Simply leading the charge into unknown territory is partly what points researchers toward certain topics.

Many of the scientific advancements we rely on were the result of unexpected outcomes to science experiments. That's not to suggest that this is the inevitable outcome of all science. But science is about exploration and discovery, so it's hard to say what is "necessary" or not. What we can all do collectively is support researchers of all disciplines, and encourage *interdisciplinary* study. This refers to researchers of separate disciplines — such as education and engineering — collaborating on research together.

(If you haven't seen the movie *Arrival* yet, this is my official recommendation to go watch it. Not only is it a beautiful film, but it shows the importance of interdisciplinary research in a very unique way.)

This chapter is a bit more theoretical than the others, but it's part of helping you think differently about research. The questions of the future will require creative problem solving, so who's to say that a study about dance won't unlock more secrets of the universe?

LESSON ACTIVITY

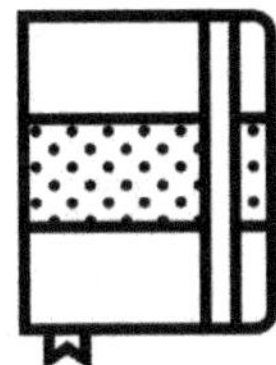

PART 1:

What is a topic you think researchers should investigate? See if you can find an existing study on it. If you can't find one, why do you think that is?

PART 2:

For a fun thought experiment, think of the potential chain of research questions that could originate from one topic. Start with a study you've found. What additional questions does it inspire?

CHAPTER 5
FOLLOW THE MONEY

To recap, research topics are often impacted by:

Industry demand;
Unexplored territory; and
Potential long-term impact.

To explore this further, we'll talk in more depth about industry demand: how research is funded.

Knowing where research originates is vital in measuring a study's credibility and impact. There are two parts to this topic: where the funding comes from, and how this impacts research.

But there's also a question that I hear frequently:
Why does research *need* funding?

The answer is simple: research is a profession like any other, which means those who do it need to make a living and support their families. Science is not just an abstraction; it has a real, tangible impact on our lives every day. Funding helps cover peoples' time, expertise, and supplies needed for the study (including materials, laboratories, technology, travel, and so on).

Many researchers are affiliated with a university or institute, serving as professors or full-time research faculty. However, their base income usually doesn't cover separate expenses that arise during a study, requiring the need for additional funding.

While many researchers would love to conduct research without worrying about money, it's the reality. (It helps when society can see it as a worthy investment.)

WHERE FUNDING COMES FROM

Research is funded in two ways: through public grants and institutions, or by private people/organizations. (To start, I recommend reading the excellent article by Boston University as part of their "Making Research Work" series: "Who picks up the tab for science?")

PUBLIC FUNDING

Public funding refers to funding from the government, often through the form of grants or scholarships. Government-funded research means that researchers are provided with government funding for their studies, or the research is conducted *by* the government. Many countries have a state "research council," such as the National Science Foundation in the United States.

PRIVATE FUNDING

Private funding refers to funding that comes from private organizations, such as non-profits, industries, corporations, professional organizations, and philanthropists. Like public funding, this often means that the research itself is conducted by members of these groups, but outside researchers can also be awarded with funding like this. Private funders of research include groups like SpaceX.

A NEWER OPTION: CROWDFUNDING

Some researchers are choosing to have their projects publically crowdfunded (which is technically an offshoot of "private" funding). Experiment.com, for example, is a crowdfunding platform specifically for scientific research. Anyone can browse the projects there, and contribute to the projects that need funding. This is a great way for researchers of all levels make their studies a reality, and helps them branch outside of what the current "demand" may be in their field.

HOW DOES FUNDING IMPACT RESEARCH?

I highly recommend reading a great piece by UC Berkeley called, "Who pays for science?" It's undeniable that funding, regardless of its source, can make a difference in the research process, methods, and outcomes. How does this work when research scientists must adhere to strict ethical rules? (We'll discuss research ethics in the coming chapters.)

In a perfect world, money wouldn't matter — all scientific studies (regardless of funding source) would be completely objective. But of course, in the real world, funding may introduce biases — for example, when the backer has a stake in the study's outcome. A pharmaceutical company paying for a study of a new depression medication, for example, might influence the study's design or interpretation in ways that subtly favor the drug that they'd like to market. There is evidence that some biases like this do occur. Drug research sponsored by the pharmaceutical industry is more likely to end up favoring the drug under consideration than studies sponsored by government grants or charitable organizations. Similarly, nutrition research sponsored by the food industry is more likely to end up favoring the food under consideration than independently funded research.

— "Who pays for science?"

The same can be said for public funding, although that tends to — historically — have a much more stringent review process than private funding. In an extreme bias-impact scenario, a university could encourage its researchers to claim breakthroughs that may be overstated, to ensure that the university gets credit for the science and/or maintains funding.

But, to clarify: funding is a vital part of research, regardless of the source. However, it's important to know the source and think critically about how it may impact the science in some way.

What's great is that much of these concerns can be mitigated through peer review. (Peer review is when other researchers in the field read and review a study and its data to ensure that the methods were optimal and the results are well-supported.) Through peer review, bias is identified and can be corrected for future studies on the topic.

LESSON ACTIVITY

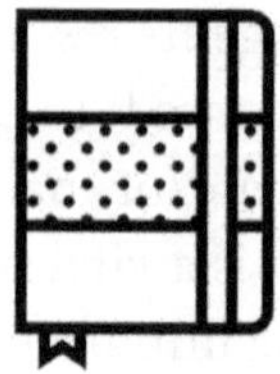

PART 1:

Find an article on a topic of your choice in a research publication. See if you can easily identify the source of the funding. Look up the funding institution. Can you tell if the study was publically or privately funded?

PART 2:

Visit Experiment.com and peruse some of the proposed projects. Are there any that you would contribute to? Do they include enough information in their pitch to convey what their research questions and methods are?

INTERVIEW WITH A RESEARCHER

NAME:
Dana Witwicki
ROLE:
Ecologist
AFFILIATION:
National Park Service,
Inventory and Monitoring
Division

How is research a part of your job?

My main role is leading long-term monitoring of dryland plants in national parks in the northern Colorado Plateau region, primarily in Utah and western Colorado. Long-term monitoring is similar to research in that you take lots of detailed measurements to understand the ecology of plants and their ecosystems, but our goal is to keep these measurements going for many decades so that we can detect changes over time and figure out why changes are occurring. Most research only lasts one to five years and has definitive questions in mind. The research questions that we look at with long-term monitoring may change over time as vegetation shifts with changes in climate or with other disturbances.

What is your educational and professional background?

I have a B.S. in Biology and a M.S. in Environmental Science. I worked in a few university labs assisting with plant ecology research early in my career. This was great experience, but ultimately I decided I wanted to be in a position where my work could directly help influence land management decisions. Working with natural resources in the national parks was a great way to do this.

What are your team's favorite research tools?

Our favorite tools are all small and lightweight since we sometimes need to carry them on long hikes to remote locations. We have a laser pointer on a monopod that we use to determine the cover of plants and small boxes containing a kit to sample the stability of the soil surface. Our crews also carry all sorts of basic measuring tools, like transect tapes, foldable rulers, and diameter tapes, that they use to set up plots and measure plants. Our heaviest tools are our electronics — a ruggedized field laptop for recording data, a GPS for navigating and collecting location data, and a camera for taking repeat photos.

I decided I wanted to be in a position where my work could directly help influence land management decisions.

What type of research does your team conduct?

As I mentioned earlier, my main responsibility is long-term monitoring of vegetation in the dryland parts of national parks in my region. This covers a wide range of elevations and vegetation types, from semi-arid grasslands and desert shrublands in the lowest and hottest areas, to sagebrush shrublands, pinyon juniper woodlands, aspen and mixed conifer forests, and finally subalpine meadows at the highest elevations. For all of these vegetation types, we are concerned about declines associated with drought and higher temperatures. We are also concerned about exotic species that can cause large changes in how ecosystems function, such as increases in the frequency of fires. One of the goals of long-term monitoring is to detect gradual changes (for example, cover of an important plant species is declining) and figure out why these changes are occurring so that park managers can determine the best ways to respond.

[Publishing] is an important way to share our work with the ecological community.

How do you evaluate the impact of your research?

The main way that we evaluate the impact of our work is by how much parks can use the information to make meaningful changes to the way they manage their land. To do this well, we need to communicate with park resource managers about their needs and incorporate this into the way that we collect and analyze data. We also need to focus on specific areas of concern within the parks that resource managers want to know more about. The other way that we evaluate success is by publishing our work in scientific journals. This is an important way to share our work with the ecological community so that we can have an impact outside of the parks as well. We usually need to look at regional patterns for this type of work (as opposed to smaller areas within parks), and our long-term data set is a great resource for doing this.

Can you share some insight into the process of publishing research?

We publish our work in a range of formats with the goal of reaching researchers, land managers, and other people outside of these fields interested in science happening in the parks. Our technical reports are targeted primarily for park resource managers while our journal articles are intended for researchers and may be useful to resource managers as well. Additionally, we publish briefs (one to four page summaries) of our work to share with a broader audience. I believe that reaching out to this broader audience is especially important and is a step that often gets left out when scientists publish their research.

How can a citizen researcher learn more about what you do?

There are a number of ways that you can learn about science happening in the National Park Service (NPS), and the website is a good place to start (nps.gov). Many of the NPS Inventory and Monitoring networks also aim to share their science with non-scientists. On our webpage, under Reports and Publications, we have a Briefs and Multimedia section with videos and printable briefs that describe the work that we do.

CHAPTER 6
PRIMUM NON NOCERE

Do you know the story of Henrietta Lacks? You may have heard of the book, *The Immortal Life of Henrietta Lacks* by Rebecca Skloot, or the movie of the same name.

Henrietta Lacks — whose birth name was Loretta Pleasant — was a young black woman who sought treatment for cancer at Johns Hopkins Hospital in 1951. Cells from her cancer biopsy led to the development of the HeLa cell line, which has led to incredible medical breakthroughs, including advancements in gene mapping and in vitro fertilization. The HeLa cells are still in use today, and have essentially been mass produced for a variety of uses.

Henrietta Lacks would never know the impact her cells made on the world. She died in October 1951, at age 31, from the cancer for which she had sought treatment. And her family, too, wouldn't know the impact she had made until well into the 1970s. At the time, scientists didn't need to ask for permission to use her cells for research, and there was no expectation to hide the identity of the cells. (I recommend reading interviews with author Rebecca Skloot, as well as first-hand accounts by Lack's family.)

It's an important story that raises many questions about research ethics.

Henrietta Lacks

WHAT ARE RESEARCH ETHICS?

Research ethics are guidelines that researchers follow to minimize harm or suffering, ensure the privacy and consent of participants, and prevent bias or conflict of interest. (The title of this chapter is Latin for "Do No Harm," which medical students agree to as part of the Hippocratic Oath.)

Research ethics is a huge topic with an ugly, often ghastly, history. You may be familiar with the Nuremberg Code, which arose from the Nuremberg trials after WWII. The Nuremberg Code was a response to the highly unethical, torturous research that Nazis conducted on victims of the Holocaust.

Another well-known research ethics code is the Belmont Report, which was created by the National Commission for the Protection of Human Subjects of Biomedical and Behavioral Research. (This commission was established as part of the 1974 National Research Act.) There are many similarities between these two sets of rules such as full consent for participation, respect for the autonomy of participants, and the right to privacy.

These documents are specifically about research on humans (physical and psychological). But research ethics impact every type of research, from history to archaeology to environmental conservation, and no study can be conducted without taking ethics into consideration.

HOW RESEARCHERS ENSURE ETHICAL STUDIES

Researchers who are affiliated with institutions have to follow very specific ethics protocol: submitting their research plans to an institutional review board (IRB) prior to conducting their study. Any study that involves humans in any way must be approved by the IRB, which is an independent committee who evaluates a study for any potential ethical problems that may arise. A researcher cannot proceed with their study until they have revised it to comply with ethics guidelines.

According to the American Psychological Association, there are five recommendations that can help researchers conduct ethical research:

1. Clearly establish, with your research team, who will get authorship credit for the research.

2. Consider conflicts of interest, or relationships with members of the study that could create bias or impact the data.

3. Follow established rules and ethics codes.

4. Respect the privacy and confidentiality of your participants.

5. Be open about your ethics concerns, and seek advice from other researchers.

RESEARCH ETHICS IN THE ERA OF BIG DATA

New questions about research ethics arise all the time, especially as technology advances. Who owns and can access the data collected on people on a daily basis?

A couple years ago, Facebook came under fire for studying its users and running experiments without user consent. Scientists argued that Facebook changed the moods of its participants, and didn't give them an opportunity to opt in or out.

This has led many to question: Are research ethics obsolete in the era of Big Data?[*] For instance, who oversees studies conducted by marketing agencies or social media platforms? Or the research done by citizen scientists? How is accountability handled when the research process is faster than ever before?

Many researchers, myself included, think that peer review can help alleviate some of these concerns. Like I discussed in the lesson about funding, peer review means that others in the same field or industry review a study to help eliminate potential bias or misleading results. Peer review helps hold researchers accountable every step of the way. The challenge is getting everyone to participate in peer review.

One thing is for sure: research ethics are complicated, and will continue to become more complicated as we move into the future.

Check out this article by Forbes: https://www.forbes.com/sites/kalevleetaru/2016/06/17/are-research-ethics-obsolete-in-the-era-of-big-data/

LESSON ACTIVITY

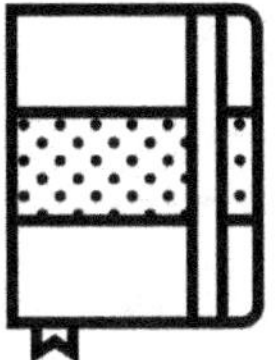

PART 1:

Think of a topic you would be interested in studying. What ethical questions could arise? Consider your relationship to the topic; are there any conflicts of interest that would occur if you were the one conducting the research?

PART 2:

Find a study on a topic that interests you. Do the researchers disclose their ethical process?

CHAPTER 7
THE HERO'S QUEST
(PART 1)

Are you familiar with the myth of Jason and the Golden Fleece?

It's an old Greek myth about Jason, son of King Aeson of Iolcos. Jason and the Argonauts (sailors aboard the *Argo*) go in search of fleece from a gold-hair winged ram. The journey is difficult, and Jason obtains the mythical material. (Par for the course in Greek mythology, additional tragedy occurs.)

This tale has become an allegory for a quest that involves a difficult search. Have you noticed that many myths and fairytales are about searching for something?

Are you ready to embark on your hero's quest?

We're going to delve into one of my absolute favorite topics: searching for, and finding, research.

Back in chapter three, we talked about access, but we're taking that to the next level. By now, you've learned:

- How to look for sources;
- How to determine if a source is credible;
- How a research article is structured;
- How research topics are determined;
- How research can be accessed;
- How research is funded;
- What research ethics are (and why they're important.)

With this knowledge, I think you're ready to start being a savvier hunter, and learn how to navigate through actual research databases. I've found that introductory research courses tend to start with this topic, rather than build up to it. However, my philosophy is that it's more important to be a critical reader of research than an expert finder of it.

This topic is broken up into two parts: finding research using digital tools, and finding research using analog tools. In this chapter, we're discussing effective search strategies for search engines and library databases.

USING SEARCH ENGINES EFFECTIVELY

So much of our lives are connected to the web, and I *truly deeply* believe that knowing how to use a search engine efficiently is a vital skill. (I even used two adverbs in a row just now; my former editors are shaking their heads in shame.)

Essentially, a search engine is a web-based aggregator of content and information. Input a search term, or "keyword," and it will give you results based on that keyword. Google is the big one, but it's certainly not the only one. Regardless, they all work more or less the same. Keep in mind that there are algorithms at play that do affect what appears in search results (such as paid ads, or your own search history).

TIPS FOR USING SEARCH ENGINES

Be as specific as possible. You can always get more general if you're not getting desired results, but it pays off to be very specific in your search request. For instance, if you're looking for information about "red wine made in Rome," start with that rather than just plugging in "Italian wine."

Be mindful of spelling. Search engines are smart, but if your input isn't correct, it can only give you what you ask for. I can't tell you how often I used to help people at the university library who were upset they couldn't find what they were looking for — because their keyword was misspelled. It happens!

Use filtering or advanced search tools. This helps to further refine your results, especially for topics that yield hundreds or thousands of results. Every search engine offers the ability to filter your results by time or relevancy. On Google, you can select "tools" to bring up these options:

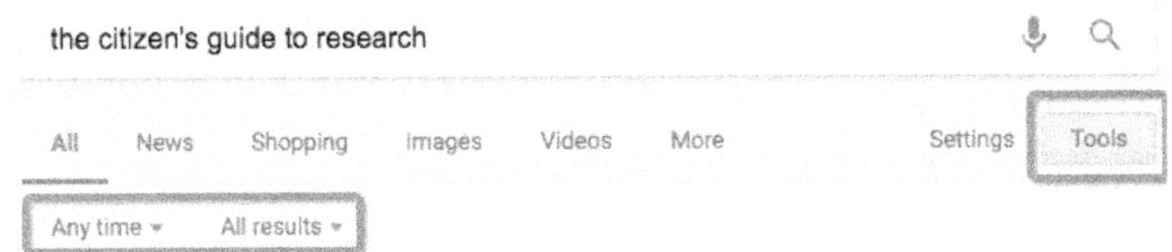

Google Scholar

If you want to use Google to access published research, you can use Google Scholar, which is a mix of Google and a traditional research database. This is a great way to narrow your search to research publications, but keep in mind that not all of the content found on it has been peer reviewed. You should still apply all of the same credibility standards on the articles you find there.

USING A LIBRARY DATABASE

A library database is an archive of information — research journals, newspapers, photographs, audio/video, and more. Popular library databases include:

WorldCat.org
JSTOR.org
EBSCO.com

Libraries pay to have access to these databases, which means that you, too, can access the information in them. University libraries tend to have access to more databases.

Try visiting one of these databases. You'll see their main homepage, and a search bar. You can certainly start there, but I recommend instead clicking "Advanced Search." On World-Cat, this takes you a page with this:

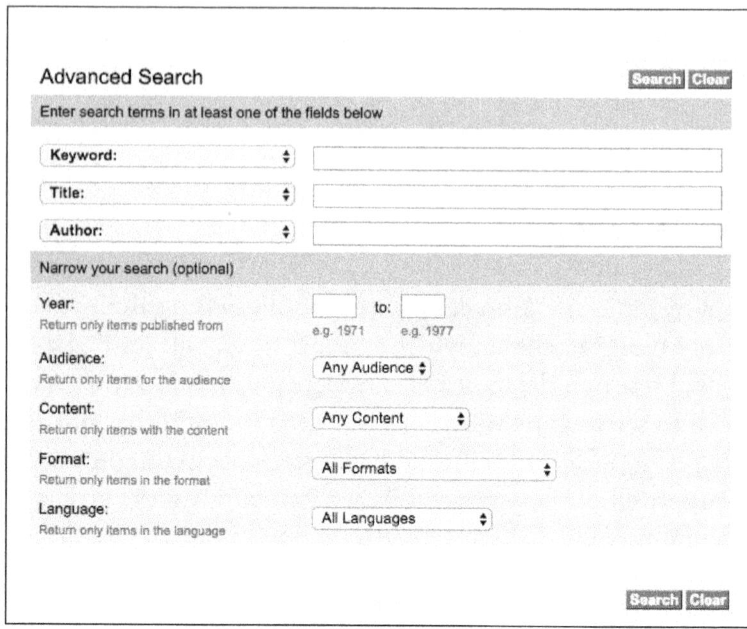

The more you can fill out here, the better. It's OK if you don't have all the pieces yet.

KEYWORDS

You can use a keyword field to start searching for your topic. The keywords are just the variables that the database uses to find you results. You can try various keywords. For instance, I may try "Cassinasco Italy" to start — maybe there's a popular book about the location that will appear first — and then refine my search further by dates.

You can use multiple keywords by separating them by commas.

Cassinasco, Italy, history

BOOLEAN TERMS

This term refers to the words: AND, NOT, and OR.

If you use the word AND to link two search terms — for example, *Cassinasco* and *1850* — your search results will only include results about both Cassinasco and 1850. Using OR means that the results will include one or both of the terms; your results may be about Cassinasco, or about Northern Italy, or about both. If you use OR, you'll want to use comparable terms. For example, Cassinasco and 1850 don't work with this, because you may get results about 1850 that are unrelated to Cassinasco.

Using NOT means that the search engine will only find results for the first term. You can use this to specify your results even further.

You can use these all in conjunction, along with parenthesis, which will designate what is searched first. For instance, I may search:

(Cassinasco Italy) AND **1800s** AND **daily life**

Remember that your goal is to find research that directly pertains to the topic you're searching for. While it may seem like a good thing to get thousands of results, it means that you have much more to wade through. Instead, focus on getting fewer results that are more specific. You want *quality* over *quantity*.

LESSON ACTIVITY

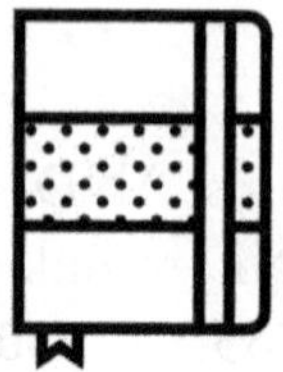

PART 1:

Go to Google Scholar and search for an article on a topic you like. How many results come up from your first search? How can you refine it further to get fewer results?

PART 2:

Visit WorldCat or another one of the databases listed above. Try searching for the same topic. Do you see similar results? What can you do to refine your search?

CHAPTER 8
THE HERO'S QUEST
(PART II)

Ask any librarian or history buff about the Library of Alexandria, and I bet you their expression will be one of sorrow or lamentation.

The Library of Alexandria was an ancient library in Alexandria, Egypt, and it was destroyed in two separate attacks (by Julius Caesar's army and Aurelian, respectively). Constructed in 3 B.C., it was one of the most prolific libraries ever established at that point in human history, hosting thousands and thousands of scrolls containing ideas, musings, observations and understandings of the world. Its destruction is still bitter to those who wonder: what did we lose when the Library of Alexandria was destroyed?

Luckily, there is some historian consensus that much of the information housed in the library was moved to other facilities, so it's possible that not as much was lost as initially believed.

But this prompts the question: what role does print and analog still play in a digital era?

We're in an unprecedented era of digital information. In many ways, this is wonderful, as information and science has become much more accessible to people around the world. It's hard to argue the positive impact of ebooks and digitized data.

But many researchers still see immense value in print information — for instance, original handwritten documents, photographs, or maps — and any savvy citizen researcher should still have the skills to navigate through institutions of print or analog information.

UNDERSTANDING LIBRARY CATALOGUING SYSTEMS

In this chapter, we're continuing our lesson about finding research. When is the last time you visited your local library?

Depending on the type of library you visited (a university library, for example), the call system (or classification system) you used to find information may vary. Two of the most common classification systems are the Dewey Decimal System (DDC) and the Library of Congress (LC or LoC). These systems were named after their originators: Melvil Dewey, who created the DDC in 1876, and the Library of Congress, which established the LC system.

(There are more classification systems, many of which are specific to countries or languages; however, these are likely the ones you will encounter in the U.S).

According to the National Library Board, the differences between these two systems is based on library size:

— National Library Board

When you're planning a research visit to a library, visit their
website or call to see which classification they use. Libraries
also have classification references, often right on the shelves,
to help guide your search. Check the guide in the back of the
book for a full list of DDC and LC call numbers.

Your research visit will also depend on what type of media
you're looking for. Print resources (besides books) you may
encounter include:

- Maps
- Photographs
- Microfiche
- Encyclopedias
- Films
- Recorded audio
- Print journals
- Magazines
- Physical items (such as pieces of art, archaeological find-
  ings, etc.)

These items are often housed in different parts of a library,
and some may require librarian assistance (such as using a
microfiche machine).

VISITING SPECIALTY LIBRARIES AND MUSEUMS

Not all libraries house a general collection of materials. Many institutions are specialty or niche facilities, which means they specialize in a topic or field.

Visiting a library or museum with a dedicated interest is really helpful when doing research. Not only do you have access to information directly related to your topic, but the librarians or curators who work there are specialists, too.

For example, New York City alone has more than 50 specialty libraries and museums, including:

- General Society of Mechanics and Tradesmen Library
- Lesbian Herstory Archives
- Museum of Sex
- Conjuring Arts (about, yes, magic)
- Museum of Mathematics

If your research interests are in a niche field, libraries and museums in the same field can help guide your research without having to wade through everything else.

CONDUCTING RESEARCH ABROAD

Even with the wealth of information online, many researchers still travel for work; not all libraries or museums have digital catalogs, and some resources simply must be visited in person. As you can imagine, this presents some unique challenges, especially if you travel to places that use languages other than your own.

Some recommendations for conducting research abroad:

Keep a translation app handy. While a translation app doesn't replace the benefit of having an actual human translator, it can help alleviate some of the stress of navigating through a foreign catalog. Google's translation app, for example, can translate words in real time using your phone camera.

Study their cataloguing system. Like I mentioned earlier, classification systems vary internationally, so this is one thing you can study ahead of time to be more prepared when you get there.

Reach out ahead of time. Communicate with researchers, locals, or scholars in the region you're visiting. They may offer to help with translation, or help you navigate through local collections.

Document your findings the best you can. If you're visiting a library or museum temporarily, it's unlikely you'll be able to bring their resources back with you. Be ready to document your findings thoroughly: take pictures, scan documents, and record ideas so that you don't miss anything when you return home.

WORKING WITH LIBRARIANS

It's important to remember the most valuable part about doing research in libraries vs. online: librarians! Librarians are experts at finding information; this is why their profession requires a Master's degree, at the very least. Specialists tend to have additional degrees in the field of their choosing.

Be specific. Librarians are smart, but they're not mind readers. Share with them specific information for what you're seeking: topic, author, title, etc.

Be transparent. They are there to help you, so be clear with what you research question is. They can direct you to resources you may not have considered.

Be respectful of their expertise. I'll never forget when a teacher said to me, "I thought librarians were like cashiers." A librarian is not just someone who puts books on a shelf (and those who do reshelve books also deserve respect!); librarians are researchers in their own right, and they know their library's collection better than anyone. This knowledge is invaluable to fellow researchers.

Take care of their library. When you're visiting a library, be kind to their resources; don't write in books, break machinery, or make a mess. Libraries serve many people, so be a nice patron.

There are many stereotypes about who librarians are: stuffy old ladies with lots of cats and no sense of humor. That couldn't be farther from the truth. People who become librarians come from diverse backgrounds and interests, and are linked by a passion for information and learning.

LESSON ACTIVITY

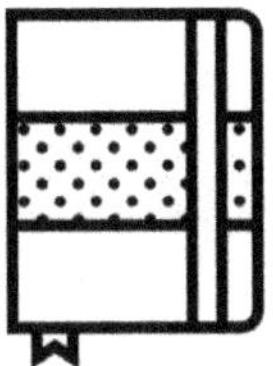

PART 1:

Go to your local library! Get a library card, if you don't currently have one. Introduce yourself to a librarian. Get to know the lay of the land.

PART 2:

Find a piece of research on a topic of your choosing that isn't a book or a journal (such as a map or an artifact). What can you learn from this unique item? Does it convey anything different or new about your chosen topic?

INTERVIEW WITH A LIBRARIAN

NAME:
Jason Puckett
ROLE:
Online Learning Librarian/
Anthropology Librarian
AFFILIATION:
Georgia State University

What is your educational and professional background?

I've got a Bachelor's degree in English from Georgia State — where I now work as a librarian — and a Master of Science in Library and Information Studies from Florida State. I've worked in libraries for over twenty years now, the last nine as a degreed librarian and as support staff before that. I've spent the last eight years as a subject librarian at GSU, meaning I support the work of specific academic departments, help with their research, buy books in their subjects for the library, teach research classes and so on.

What drew you to librarianship?

I kind of fell into it accidentally at first. I had a tech support background, got a job doing computer support in an academic library, and gradually shifted from that into reference staff positions. Eventually I went to library school when I decided that was what I wanted to do for a profession. I've always enjoyed the research process, writing papers in school, so making that a focus of my career was a natural fit.

What do you imagine libraries will be like in the future?

There will always be a lot of familiar elements to the library. Print books are such a perfect format in so many ways that they'll never go away. We're just going to keep adding to them as we discover new ways to make and manipulate and share information. What's been interesting to me over the last few years is seeing what form those changes are starting to take — my library now has a VR room and 3D scanners and printers, which are not things I'd ever have thought of as being within the library's purview.

> *We're just going to keep adding to [libraries] as we discover new ways to make and manipulate and share information.*

As someone who works with researchers, what do you think are the most important skills a researcher should have?

Researching online is like drinking from a fire hose. We're inundated with information. Distinguishing useful sources from bad ones is both difficult and crucial. In academic research, we use the concept of peer review — basically, determining whether information holds up as valid under knowledgeable scrutiny — as one of our main filters, but that's sometimes tricky to do in daily life. There's a method that a lot of librarians teach undergrads called the CRAAP test: look at a source's currency, relevance, accuracy, authority, and purpose as you decide whether it's reliable and useful. Some version of this, even if it's just having a healthy skepticism in the back of one's mind, is really key.

What are your favorite research tools?

I use and teach a citation manager application called Zotero that's just great. It lets you save citations for sources you're using, and generates bibliographies in a couple of clicks. I tell students it's like iTunes for citations — you can organize them, attach PDFs and notes, and save all the information you need to cite it in a paper. And it's free! If you're really interested, look for my book *Zotero: A Guide for Librarians, Researchers, and Educators* at your library.

Distinguishing useful sources from bad ones is both difficult and crucial.

What do you recommend to a citizen researcher who wants to improve their research skills in every day life?

I mentioned peer review earlier, which is when academic research gets scrutinized by other experts before it's accepted for publication — this is how scholarly journals try to make sure that they're publishing reliable information. It's easy to do a "light" version of this in non-professional research by making sure the research source you're looking at is backed up by other sources. Snopes.com is a great example of this; they don't make unsubstantiated claims and they show where all their information came from.

What else do you want people to know about libraries?

Just that reference librarians are here to help. It's our job! A lot of our college students don't realize that there's a support system in place to help with their research, especially early in their academic careers. It's true whether you're at a university doing academic research, or at your public library doing personal research.

CHAPTER 9
CITATION STATION

Do you remember the Schoolhouse Rock song that goes, "Conjunction junction, what's your function?" I used to sing a similar version to my English 101 students; mine went, "Citation station, if it's not your creation!" It embarrassed them (I have no shame) but it was a silly way to make light of a topic that can be tedious.

In this chapter, we'll discuss what citation is, how citation styles differ, and why it's important to cite. You may remember some of this information from high school or college. But it's helpful to remember that citations aren't just nitpicky preferences of your English teachers; citation is a necessary part of how the research world works and progresses.

WHAT DOES IT MEAN TO CITE SOMETHING?

To cite is to attribute an idea, concept, or quote to its original author or creator. Contrary to popular belief, citation isn't solely about "credit" (although that's a big part of it). All research is part of a larger conversation, and citing helps distinguish between existing and new ideas.

CITATION STYLES

From school, you may remember hearing about "MLA style" or "APA style." When I was teaching, many of my students weren't sure about what this all meant, and what the differences were. Here's a quick primer of some of the more popular citation styles used in major colleges and universities:

- **AMERICAN PSYCHOLOGICAL ASSOCIATION (APA):** Used in social sciences and education. According to Mercer University, this style is "well-suited to qualitative studies and analysis."
- **AMERICAN ANTHROPOLOGICAL ASSOCIATION (AAA):** Used in anthropological research.
- **MODERN LANGUAGE ASSOCIATION (MLA):** Used in humanities and literature research. According to Mercer University, this style is "well-suited to literature and archival sources."
- **CHICAGO/TURABIAN STYLE:** Used in business, history, and some art research.
- **NATIONAL LIBRARY OF MEDICINE (NLM):** Used in medical research. (Some medical research may use APA style.)
- **IEEE (INSTITUTE OF ELECTRICAL AND ELECTRONICS ENGINEERS):** Used in engineering science and research.

WHY ARE THERE SO MANY DIFFERENT STYLES?

Mercer University's excellent resource on citations says it best:

> It might seem like academic authors can't agree, but really, authors write for different purposes and different audiences, and so the citation styles reflect that.
>
> We continue to use different citation styles for two main reasons: disciplinary differences and tradition. Researchers in different disciplines cite different types of resources, and different disciplines place higher value on different criteria. For example, most researchers in the social sciences are more likely to cite a scholarly article than any other type of source, while a researcher in the humanities might need to cite a variety of source types, including archived personal letters or first-edition works. Over time, organizations like the American Psychological Association created style guides that were meant to help standardize the format of citations within their discipline, focused on the types of works most often used in their field.

WHAT CITATIONS LOOK LIKE

Within a study, you'll see citations in two different ways: in-text citations, and a reference (or works cited) page. The formatting of each of these will vary, depending on the style of the research article. An in-text citation is an attribution that appears directly within the body of the article. A reference page is a list, usually alphabetical, of all of the works mentioned within the article.

An in-text citation may look like an author's name, or a title, in parenthesis at the end of a sentence. On a reference page, a citation usually includes the author, the name of their work, the date of publishing, and additional information, such as the publisher. Here's an example of an MLA style citation:

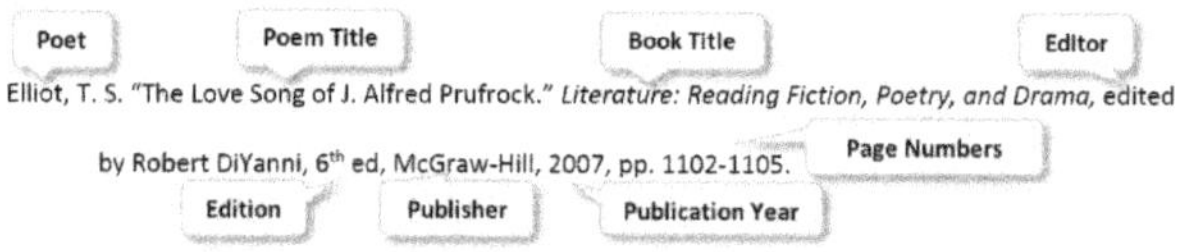

TOOLS TO HELP WITH CITATIONS

Many people, researchers and students alike, struggle with writing accurate citations; there's a lot to remember about formatting, down to where to place commas or periods.

To help with this, there are tools that can "generate" a reference to add to a reference page. Plug in information, and it will generate a citation. While these tools should be used in conjunction with style guides, they can help you with the basics.

Here are a few of the more popular citation tools:
- EasyBib
- Citation Machine
- BibMe
- Cite This For Me

WHY DOES CITATION MATTER TO CITIZEN RESEARCHERS?

It may seem like citation is just another aspect of published research that seems stuffy and finicky, but it serves an important purpose — not just for researchers, but for those who read research and seek to apply it to real-world questions. Remember when we discussed credibility, and identifying the source? Citation is the system that helps us do that.

We may not use structured citations when we share research and discuss it outside of academia, but the concept is the same. Citation provides some semblance of credibility, as it shows that the researcher has included topical information and ideas from others, and is acknowledging that in their new research. It's also a way for researchers to gauge the impact of their studies, by seeing where their work is cited and how it's been applied to different questions.

LESSON ACTIVITY

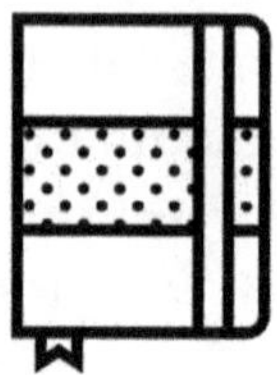

PART 1:

Find an article on a topic you like. Go to the reference page or works cited page. Can you identify what citation style is in use? (Tip: Think about the *topic* of the article and how this may impact the citation style.)

PART 2:

Identify something on the reference page that seems interesting to you. Use the citation to try to find the original article. Does it provide all of the information you need to find it?

To conclude Part 1, it's fitting to close with research methods before you embark on your own research. Most research can be categorized in two types: qualitative and quantitative. Just by looking at these words, you may be able to figure out what they mean, but it's not as simple as "quality" vs. "quantity."

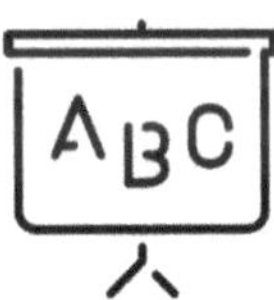

Qualitative research *refers to collecting data that isn't in "numerical" form (for instance, case studies that consist of interviews with people).*

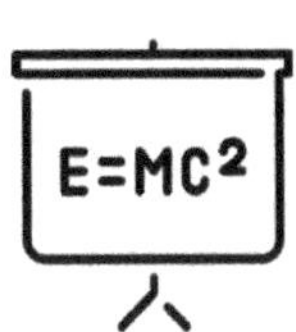

Quantitative research *refers to numerical data (for instance, temperature or census numbers).*

Some researchers conduct what's known as mixed-methods research, which can include multiple types of methodology, and can mix qualitative and quantitative.

Sometimes, the topic of research influences the type of study. For instance, many education researchers choose qualitative, especially when conducting studies in classrooms. Qualitative works best with smaller groups, whereas quantitative is preferable for large populations who are being surveyed, or datasets with many variables.

The methods of the study then impacts how it's analyzed. There are many, many ways to analyze data. Qualitative data, such as interview transcripts, may be "coded"; this means that the responses of participants will be placed into categories so the research can better understand the nature of the responses, and draw conclusions.

Quantitative data is analyzed using statistical analysis. Statistics is a fascinating topic, but can be daunting or alienating; we'll cover some common statistics in Part 2 of this series. (I strongly believe everyone should know basic stats! Don't worry; I promise it will be fun.)

WHY DOES THIS MATTER?

Knowing the different types of research, and the context in which they are used, can help you understand the logic behind research methodology. The method type is indicative of how researchers plan to address their research questions and hypotheses. One research topic can be studied and analyzed in many ways.

Researchers tend to have a preference for — and a specialty in — qualitative, quantitative, or mixed-methods.

LESSON ACTIVITY

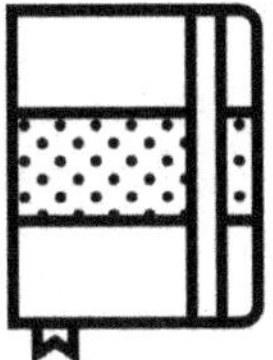

Look at the analysis section of an article you've found after a previous lesson in this book. Can you determine what type of study it is? What in the study indicates this?

INTERVIEW WITH A RESEARCHER

NAME:
Emily Lescak
ROLE:
Postdoctoral fellow
AFFILIATION:
University of Alaska-
Anchorage

How is research a part of your job?

My role is 100 percent research. I am a National Science Foundation-funded postdoc studying host-microbe interactions using threespine stickleback fish as a model organism.

What is your educational and professional background?

During my senior year at Clark University, I did a group project examining shy/bold behavior in stickleback originating from lakes with and without piscivorous fish as part of my animal behavior course. The professor invited me to do field work in Alaska with her the following summer to collect more fish and expand the project, but I was unavailable due to previous commitments. However, about six months later, my husband got a job in Alaska and I wrote my professor asking her to introduce me to her colleague at the University. He invited me to apply to be a graduate student in his lab. I completed a Masters examining stickleback morphological variation and predator-prey interactions and then a PhD focused on contemporary evolution of wild populations from earthquake-uplifted islands. In my postdoc, I am applying my background in stickleback ecology, behavior, genetics, and morphology to understand how disruptions to the gut microbiome influence physiological and behavioral development.

What are your favorite research tools?

Minnow traps!

What type of research do you conduct?

Most of my work consists of developmental experiments, in which we cross adult fish from multiple wild populations in the lab and then rear the offspring in different environments (e.g. germ-free, antibiotic exposed) and watch how they develop, focusing on various aspects of morphology (e.g. overall length, organ size) and behavior.

> *There are also a ton of really good teaching resources online that explain scientific concepts in easy-to-understand, interactive ways.*

How do you evaluate the impact of your research?

Mostly through number of citations, but also altmetrics and in some cases, media coverage.

Can you share some insight into the process of publishing research?

It's important to be patient! It is enjoyable to get reviewers who seem interested and excited about the work and suggest novel ways of thinking about it.

Being a reviewer has also greatly impacted the way I think about the structure and organization of papers and use of different writing styles.

If you know a scientist, pick their brain!

How can a citizen researcher learn more about science and research?

PBS is a great resource, with science-based programming for both kids and adults. There are also a ton of really good teaching resources online, particularly through HHMI (Howard Hughes Medical Institute) and universities, that explain scientific concepts in easy to understand, interactive ways. Researchers also do a lot of community outreach and universities will often hold events for the general public. If you know a scientist, pick their brain! They love to talk about their work.

BECOMING A CITIZEN RESEARCHER

CHAPTER 11

ASSEMBLY REQUIRED

ASSEMBLING YOUR RESEARCH TOOLKIT

Before you can start doing research, you have to assemble the tools and services you will use to help you with your research. A great tool can make research fun and easier. Your research toolkit should consist of the following:

- A word processing app or software to document your findings and write your report
- A cloud-based app to use for note-taking throughout the process
- A citation manager to handle the references you plan to use in your research

There are some other recommendations included below that I think are helpful, but at least pick three tools that meet the above criteria.

WORD PROCESSOR

Early on, pick a tool you can use to document your notes and your research. There are countless word processing programs out there, but here are some I recommend checking out:

- Microsoft Word (paid)
- Libre Office (free/open source)
- LaTeX (free)
- Emacs (free/open source)
- Scrivener (paid)
- Google Docs (free)
- Ulysses (paid)

CLOUD-BASED NOTETAKER

Along with a word processor, it's helpful to have a web version for general outlining, planning, and note-taking. Use a cloud service so you don't have to worry about losing any of your notes. Cloud notetakers tend to also offer options to upload other file types, including spreadsheets or images.

Recommended apps:
Evernote or Google Keep

CITATION MANAGER

When you start researching a topic, you will collect a ton of documents that you'll need to cite in your paper. A tool specific for this purpose is a life-saver.

Recommended apps:

- **Zotero.** Free and open source, Zotero makes it easy to manage and organize your citations and references.
- **Mendeley.** Mendeley is a web app that helps researchers organize and annotate sources. I can't speak highly enough about Mendeley; I use it for *every. project. I. work. on.* Store PDFs and files, and tag them or organize them via category. Their library is a nice, simple, searchable archive if you're looking for some additional sources to add to your study or paper (funny enough, this is how I found some of the primary sources I used for my Master's thesis). There's also a social component where you can connect with other researchers.

NOTEBOOK

While I rely heavily on digital tools, I find that having a notebook is extremely helpful at any stage of the research process. I'm a fan of Word notebooks. Like Field Notes, they are small, so I always keep one in my purse in case inspiration strikes (nothing sucks more than being stuck somewhere without something to write in!). I love the design and the feel of these notebooks. At the start of a project, I write down my goals, and I look at them again toward the end to see if I met those goals. I also track my time spent on various sources/archives, effective search terms, and annotations.

BOOKMARKING

If you're in the middle of researching a specific topic, a bookmarking tool can help you easily save the articles and content you find on that topic. My preferred tool for this is Pocket (getpocket.com). Pocket is a great way to bookmark articles, pictures, etc. that I find anywhere on the web. I can add tags to each thing I bookmark to easily organize them by topic or project. I use this instead of adding articles to my bookmark bar in my browser, as that can very quickly get overcrowded. Organization is key for a researcher, so I love tools that make it easy to stay organized!

LESSON ACTIVITY

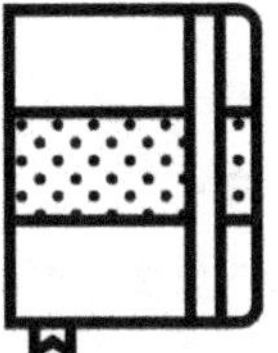

Using the list at the beginning of the lesson, pick your research tools. You might find that some of these tools are helpful for your job or hobby beyond just using them for research purposes!

CHAPTER 12
RIDDLE ME THIS

One of my favorite archetypes in fiction and folklore is that of the trickster. A trickster is a character that tends to be cryptic or sneaky. I especially love when they ensnare the protagonist in a riddle, and the protagonist must respond to the riddle to fight their way out. This is a trope that occurs often in myths or fairytales.

Determining what to research can often feel like the process of both writing and solving a riddle. Researchers want their question to be clever and thought-provoking so their data has impact. But if it's too complicated, it becomes too hard to answer, because there are too many elements to it.

Coming up with your research question — the question you are trying to answer with research and data — may seem easy, but it can actually be tricky. A research project can't begin until the research question has been established.

One thing to remember is this: a **research question** is separate from a **hypothesis**. It helps to think of your research question as, well, a *question*, and your hypothesis as a *statement*.

The Center for Innovation in Research and Teaching (CIRT) at Grand Canyon University makes a good distinction: *a research question is inquisitive, and a hypothesis is predictive.*

Here are some tips for formulating your research question.

BE SPECIFIC

When I was teaching English 101, my students had to write a research paper. Coming up with a research question never failed to stump them! The reason why: their questions weren't specific. When a research question isn't specific, it means that there is too much to answer, so the amount of research on that topic quickly becomes overwhelming. Here's an example from SUNY Empire State University:

"[If your topic is] juvenile delinquency (a topic that can be researched), you might ask the following questions:

- What is the 1994 rate of juvenile delinquency in the U.S.?
- What can we do to reduce juvenile delinquency in the U.S.?
- Does education play a role in reducing juvenile delinquents' return to crime?

Once you complete your list, review your questions in order to choose a usable one that is neither too broad nor too narrow. In this case, the best research question is 'c.' Question 'a' is too narrow, since it can be answered with a simple statistic. Question 'b' is too broad; it implies that the researcher will cover many tactics for reducing juvenile delinquency that could be used throughout the country. Question 'c,' on the other hand, is focused enough to research in some depth."

TRY REPHRASING YOUR QUESTION

If you're having a hard time making your question clear,
try rephrasing it to see if it can be refined. You can try the
journalist method of "who, what, where, how, why, when?"
Placing different words at the start of your question may illu-
minate what doesn't fit.

For instance, asking:
"Why do pets make people happy?"
is a different question than,
"Does having a pet make people happy?"
which is different than,
"How do pets contribute to personal happiness?"
etc. etc.

The basis for all of those questions is the same, but rephrasing
it provides a different research process for each one.

DETERMINE WHAT TYPE OF QUESTION YOU'RE ASKING

Rephrasing your question also helps you to figure out what
type of question you're asking.

The type of question you're asking impacts the methodology of your study — basically, how you plan to conduct your
research and analyze the findings. We'll talk about methodology in the coming chapters, so don't concern yourself with
that just yet, but you can start by identifying what type of
question you're asking.

Three main types of questions:

Causal Questions – *Compares two or more phenomena and determines if a relationship exists. Often called relationship research questions. Example: Does the amount of calcium in the diet of elementary school children effect the number of cavities they have per year?*

Descriptive Questions – *Seek to describe a phenomena and often study "how much", "how often", or "what is the change". Example: How often do college-aged students use Twitter?*

Comparative Questions – *Aim to examine the difference between two or more groups in relation to one or more variables. The questions often begin with "What is the difference in...". Example: What is the difference in caloric intake of high school girls and boys?*

- Center for Innovation in Research and Teaching

ADDITIONAL CONSIDERATIONS

Here are a few additional things to keep in mind when formulating your research question:

Is it feasible to research?

Some questions are much harder than others to research. Does your question seem accessible for you with your existing resources, or does your question require tools, people, or resources out of reach? This doesn't mean your question isn't worth pursuing, but it may be a topic you investigate in depth over time, rather than just with one research report.

Does your question bring something new to the topic/ field?

Has your question been answered in some way already? Many topics have been researched in depth, so you may find your question answered already by other researchers. Don't get discouraged if this is the case. You may discover that rephrasing your question brings something new to the table. And it's good practice to try researching a well-established topic to see if your findings are aligned with the consensus within that field.

LESSON ACTIVITY

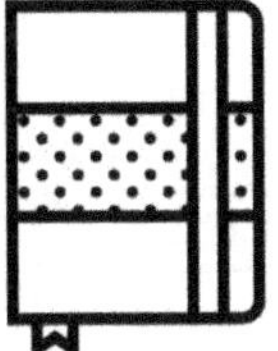

This lesson marks the start of you working through your own research project. By the end of the book, my hope is that you have something to share with your friends and family.

To start, pick your research question. Base it on a topic you are passionate about. Don't worry about how you're going to answer it just yet. Follow the rules in this chapter for refining your research question. Then, ask yourself this:

- Is it specific?
- What type of research question is it?
- Based on my research question, what is my hypothesis?

CHAPTER 13
POINT OF (RE)VIEW

You know the old adage, "Imitation is the sincerest form of flattery"? In a way, research *kind* of works like that — in the sense that nearly all research builds upon the research of others. This doesn't mean that researchers simply copy the work of others, but it's important that research is reproduced by others so that findings can be replicated, and theories can be formed around those findings.

It's also necessary for researchers to credit the discoveries of others. As I've said before, research is all part of a great conversation, so it helps to know where ideas originate.

In this chapter, we're going to talk about writing a literature a review. A literature review is the part of a research paper where the researcher analyzes existing research relevant to the new study. According to the UC Santa Cruz Library, "The purpose is to offer an overview of significant literature published on a topic." It's not quite a book report, but it has a similar concept. It's the researcher's job to read through a bunch of books and research articles, and to extract the main points and themes that are found within all of this information. This is where citation becomes really important. To refresh your memory:

To cite is to attribute an idea, concept, or quote to its original author or creator. Contrary to popular belief, citation isn't solely about "credit" (although that's a big part of it). All research is part of a larger conversation, and citing helps distinguish between existing and new ideas.

WHY WRITE A LITERATURE REVIEW?

A literature review serves a few purposes. It helps the researcher frame their new study in the context of what has come before. What were the findings of other researchers exploring this topic?

It's also useful for the researcher to help form their research question and methodology. Exploring existing research on the topic they are interested in can help identify what still needs to be studied. It also influences the methodology and analysis that may be helpful.

For example, when I was writing my thesis on cyberactivism, I noticed that many of the researchers who write about that topic use quantitative studies. Because the topic was web-based, cyberactivist researchers found that using quantitative methods and analysis was best suited to the topic, since it allowed them to survey large groups of people. This helped me see examples of how I could format my own study.

HOW TO WRITE YOUR LITERATURE REVIEW

Set up your research parameters. Be sure to include recently published research; this will more accurately reflect the topic as it's being researched now. You may choose to incorporate one or two older works, to lay the foundation of your topic, but newer research will better help you identify what in the topic still needs to be investigated.

Plan your reading schedule. There's no consensus about how many citations a research report needs, but for some context, a Master's thesis should aim for around 40 references. That's a lot of research to read, and research can be dense. A literature review should take several weeks to complete, so plan to tackle a little bit every day.

Select your citation manager. If you haven't already explored the tools I discussed a few chapters ago, be sure to find a citation manager you love. Dealing with 40+ PDFs, files, or books can be overwhelming; every study I do results in a massive file, or a massive pile, of books or articles. Start organizing early so you don't get overwhelmed. I love using tools like Mendeley or Zotero for this purpose.

Create an outline using themes you recognize. The best place to start actually writing the review is to create a simple outline by theme. For example, when I was reading through research about cyberactivism, themes I noticed were:
- Differences in opinion based on age;
- Different types of mediums used (forums, online petitions, social media);
- Different approaches to literacy.

These themes helped me frame which studies I wanted to talk about in each section of my literature review.

Literature reviews should comprise the following elements:

- *An overview of the subject, issue or theory under consideration, along with the objectives of the literature review*
- *Division of works under review into categories (e.g. those in support of a particular position, those against, and those offering alternative theses entirely)*
- *Explanation of how each work is similar to and how it varies from the others*
- *Conclusions as to which pieces are best considered in their argument, are most convincing of their opinions, and make the greatest contribution to the understanding and development of their area of research*

In assessing each piece, consideration should be given to:

Provenance—What are the author's credentials? Are the author's arguments supported by evidence (e.g. primary historical material, case studies, narratives, statistics, recent scientific findings)?
Objectivity—Is the author's perspective even-handed or prejudicial? Is contrary data considered or is certain pertinent information ignored to prove the author's point?
Persuasiveness—Which of the author's theses are most/least convincing?
Value—Are the author's arguments and conclusions convincing? Does the work ultimately contribute in any significant way to an understanding of the subject?

— Write a Literature Review, UC Santa Cruz

LESSON ACTIVITY

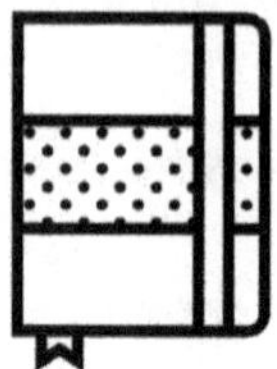

Find five pieces of research — articles in a journal, books, a news source, etc. — that are related to your research question. As you read through these, see if you can identify:

- Three main themes;
- Any consensus about findings on that topic (what do the researchers seem to agree on?);
- Similarities in analysis (can you tell how they analyzed their data?)

As we go, be sure to document everything in the word processor of your choosing.

CHAPTER 14
BY DESIGN

So, let's recap:

You've compiled your research toolkit.

You've come up with your research question and hypothesis.

You've studied existing research on the topic.

You're ready to get out there and start collecting data.

Hold up! There's an important step before you can get to the fun part. (I think data collection is the fun part. And analyzing the results. Well, all of it is the fun part!)

In this chapter, we're talking about research methodology. That word may make you want to roll your eyes; "methodology" sounds so stuffy, right? All this refers to is how you plan to collect the data that will help you answer your research question. You can also call it "research design."

In Chapter 10 of Part 1, we briefly went over research methodology — specifically, qualitative and quantitative methodology. To refresh your memory:

Most research can be categorized in two types: qualitative and quantitative. Just by looking at these words, you may be able to figure out what they mean, but it's not as simple as "quality" vs. "quantity."

Qualitative research refers to collecting data that isn't in "numerical" form (for instance, case studies that consist of interviews with people).

Quantitative research refers to numerical data (for instance, temperature or census numbers).

While most research falls into one of these categories, some methods expand on these. (For instance, ethnography is highly descriptive, so it's considered "qualitative" since it usually involves interviewing people or observing them one-on-one or in small groups.) To keep things simple, we'll stick with these two for now, but there are a lot of options for how methodology can be formed for different studies.

HOW TO DETERMINE WHAT TYPE OF METHOD WORKS FOR YOUR STUDY

Your methodology is dependent on two variables:

- Your research question
- Your literature review

Your literature review should give you some information about what type of methodology typically works best for your topic. You certainly don't have to stick to what other researchers have done in their studies, but as a researcher-in-training, this can be a great way to help you form your study.

Your research question should also be a good indicator of how you will need to collect data. An easy way to think of it is this: is your research question best answered by a large or small group of people? If you want to get data from a small group by interviewing or observing them, this would be qualitative. If you want to make a survey and collect a bunch of results, that would be quantitative.

(We're assuming here that you're researching something that has to do with people. However, many of the same ideas do apply to scientific research on non-human topics.)

The phrasing of your research question may also steer you in the right direction. This isn't a hard-and-fast rule, but questions with "why" or "how" can be most effectively answered by a few people with who you can have a more extensive conversation. If you're seeing the "what," you may want to have a lot of responses so that you can claim statistical significance (meaning, the numbers can prove a particular point. We'll talk more about that when we get to analysis).

> *"The research design refers to the overall strategy that you choose to integrate the different components of the study in a coherent and logical way, thereby, ensuring you will effectively address the research problem; it constitutes the blueprint for the collection, measurement, and analysis of data. Note that your research problem determines the type of design you should use, not the other way around!"*
>
> — De Vaus, D. A. | Research Design in Social Research

HOW YOUR METHODS AFFECT YOUR DATA COLLECTION

If choosing the right research design for your study seems complicated, don't fret! Research design takes a long time to master, and every research question offers several approaches to one study. It's very easy to go down the rabbit hole. This is why researchers study the same topic in many different ways over the course of their career; each approach gives them new insight.

You may already know what methods you want to use. Your methods affect the type of data you collect and how you will analyze it. Here are some examples of how data can be collected and analyzed within each type of methodology.

QUALITATIVE DESIGN

QUANTITATIVE DESIGN

. . . .

CONDUCTING THE STUDY

- Interviewing 5-10 people, one on one
- Observing a group of people
- Conducting a thorough case study

CONDUCTING THE STUDY

- Distributing a survey to a large group of people (more than 20)
- Testing something against two comparable groups (a variable and a control)

ANALYZING THE DATA

- Transcribing the interviews/footage
- Looking for common themes/patterns in the interviews
- Assigning a "code" for each theme
- Comparing the themes/ patterns with those found in existing studies

ANALYZING THE DATA

- Using statistical analysis to determine if results are "significant"
- Looking for correlation or relationships between variables
- Conducting a meta-analysis (essentially, a synthesis) on large subsets of existing numerical data

LESSON ACTIVITY

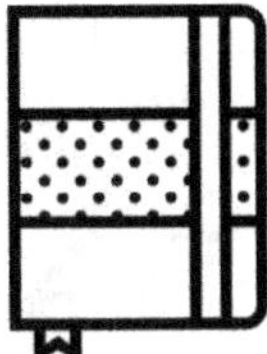

Based on your research question and the two types of research design we've discussed, do you think your study is *qualitative* or *quantitative?*

CHAPTER 15

BY THE NUMBERS (AND WORDS)

One of the most exciting parts of research is collecting data. Now that you have your research question and your methodology ready to go, the data is just going to start flowing in!

... Not. Or at least, not yet. Let's talk about data and what exactly that word means. In the next chapter, we'll talk about how to collect it.

WHAT *IS* DATA?

What do researchers mean when we talk about data? There's a common misconception that data refers solely to numerical information, but that's not entirely accurate. According to *Statistics for Dummies* (a handy manual!), "Data are the actual pieces of information that you collect through your study."

(A note for you fellow pedants: Technically, "data" is a plural word. One would use "datum" to refer to one piece of "data." As such, you could say "data are" in place of "data is." However, both uses are grammatically correct.)

Essentially, anything can serve as data, depending on what you're researching. This means that data includes:

- spreadsheets of variables;
- photographs and videos;
- audio recordings;
- maps and diagrams;
- and much more.

Remember when we talked about qualitative vs. quantitative? That's an easy way to categorize different types of data, but let's take it one step forward and explore another contrast: numerical vs. categorical.

TYPES OF NUMERICAL DATA

Numerical data can be either a measurement or a count. Let's refine further:

Discrete data: This refers to data that can be counted. (For example: how many patients a hospital treats in a year.)

Continuous data: This refers to numbers that have a range and interval. You would, in theory, be able to plot these numbers on a line. (For example: your weight, over time.)

CATEGORICAL DATA

Like the name implies, categorical data refers to information that can be categorized. For example, if you are distributing a survey that asks someone's gender, you would be collecting categories of data.

Some ask if categorical data is numerical because you can assign numbers to it. Going back to my gender example, you may have the following options:

- Male
- Female
- Non-Binary

When analyzing this data, you may assign a number to each option (1 = non-binary, 2 = female, 3 = male). However, the original data you're collecting wouldn't be numerical, because a gender isn't a "value". (We'll talk more about what it means to "code" this kind of data when we discuss analysis.)

LESSON ACTIVITY

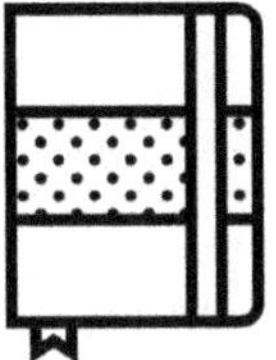

Based on your research question, what type of data do you think would best help you explore answers to that question?

INTERVIEW WITH A RESEARCHER

NAME:
Mafalda Ferreira
ROLE:
PhD Student
AFFILIATION:
Faculty of Sciences, University of Porto, Portugal

How is research a part of your job?

I'm a PhD student, currently developing my own project. As a scientist, my research has a very big component of checking old and recent literature, to be able to formulate ideas, understand if my ideas are new and fill a gap in knowledge, to find new methods or ways of interpreting my own data. The other component consists of testing my ideas and hypothesis using the scientific method and setting up experiments. Finally, as scientists, communicating is also a very big part of our research because science relies on sharing knowledge. Therefore, I also spend a large time preparing oral communications, posters and writing papers, so I'm able to share my research and results with my colleagues.

What is your educational and professional background?

I've been in the field of biology since my Bachelor's degree. Among all the topics in biology, evolution has always been a fascinating topic to me. Therefore, after having enjoyed participating in a small research project during my Bachelor program, I decided to pursue an academic career and I am currently doing my PhD at the University of Porto, Portugal.

As scientists, communicating is also a very big part of our research because science relies on sharing knowledge.

What are your favorite research tools?

For literature research, we all use Google and Google Scholar to search literature in our area. I also use PubMed or Web of Knowledge sporadically. Google is also great to solve problems, as the scientific community is great at sharing solutions for problems we all face in forums online.

What type of research does your team conduct?

We study the molecular mechanisms of evolution and adaptation, which simply means we want to understand how organisms adapt to their environment by changing their morphologic and physiologic characters through time and how that change is reflected in their genes.

How do you evaluate the impact of your research?

Like many other scientists, our research has most impact if published in high profile scientific journals and if those publications have many citations. Usually, if our research has a great impact and is meaningful, that is also reflected in the amount of funding we get.

Like many other scientists, our research has most impact if published in high profile scientific journals and if those publications have many citations.

Can you share some insight into the process of publishing research?

This process can usually take a fair bit of time and dedication. After collecting all the data, we write a draft where we show our results, interpreting them in light of previous research and discussing their implications to current knowledge. This draft circulates through all co-authors so that everyone can contribute to the text and give their insight on what was written. Then, we submit the draft to a journal we all agree is the most adequate for our manuscript, given the results we obtained and their relevance for a broader or narrower scientific audience. Then we wait. The editor of the journal must consider that our manuscript is relevant and will then send it to anonymous reviewers, that are usually chosen because they are experts in the field. We receive comments, concerns and suggestions for edits from those reviewers. If we agree with their suggestions, we change the manuscript. If not, we argue against their changes. This process goes back and forth, until the editor is satisfied with the changes we have made to the original manuscript. There is always the possibility that the editor is not satisfied and so the manuscript if refused. If that is the case, we usually revise our manuscript and submit it to another journal, going through the process again.

How can a citizen researcher learn more about science and research?

Perhaps, the best way is to talk and interact with scientists. Science communication activities, such as informal seminars, "speed-dating" (where you have ~5 min to talk with a scientist over a table) or other scientific activities and materials (books or blogs for example) directly made by scientist are preferable. I believe that scientists should also make a real effort to contact more with the public, giving interviews, visiting schools or inviting citizens to their laboratories and institutions. Contact without intermediaries is usually the best, since scientists can clarify doubts right away and pass their message directly to the public without interpretations of their results that are sometimes erroneous. •

Collecting data is really fun for both new and experienced researchers. It's super exciting to get survey responses, conduct interviews, or compile media to analyze.

WHAT TO KEEP IN MIND WHEN PICKING A COLLECTION TOOL

The way you collect data depends on the type of data you are collecting. (You're like, "Duh!" right now, I'm sure.) But different data has different considerations. Keep the following in mind when determining what tools you're going to use:

Is it secure? Will your data be encrypted or stored in a safe place? If you're collecting any personal information, it's important to have a good plan. I know researchers who lock their data in actual cabinets to ensure that it won't get lost or fall into the wrong plans. Whether you're collecting digital or analog information, consider how secure it will be.

Does it have the storage you need? Make sure that whatever tool you use is equipped to handle how much data you plan to collect. For example, if you're going to record interviews or conversations, be sure to use a storage solution that will store all of it.

Is it easy for you and your participants to use? If you're going to distribute a survey, for example, make sure the survey is easy for people to access and enter, to ensure that you can receive the most responses possible.

TOOLS FOR COLLECTING DATA

Pop quiz: What is qualitative data?

Qualitative refers to data that is non-numerical. This includes interviews, focus groups, video or audio recordings, observations, case studies, and other types of media (such as maps or photographs).

Follow-up: What's quantitative data?

Essentially, quantitative data refers to numerical data or statistical information, such as survey results or data sets with variables.

As a citizen researcher, a smartphone is an unbeatable research device. It can connect to the internet, take photos and video, and create and upload a ton of file types, so it's a wonderful tool to use for your research projects. I recommend downloading the following:

Google Drive: Google Drive is a free cloud service program that can be used to store your data to the cloud. I mentioned it in my first lesson about creating a research kit. Google Drive also consists of Google Docs, for word processing;

Google Forms, for surveys and forms; and Google Sheets, an Excel-like program. It's a must-use for citizen researchers, but keep in mind that it has some limitations for encrypted storage.

Audio Recorder: Almost every smartphone comes with a voice recorder app, but if yours doesn't, download a free one. This is perfect for recording interviews or conversations with study subjects.

Evernote/Google Keep: Having a digital notebook is always handy when researching. You may not store your data in it, but you can jot down thoughts that occur as the information comes in.

TIPS FOR COLLECTING DATA

No matter what type of data you're collecting, here are my tips for your first data collection:

Don't lead the participant: If you're conducting an interview with your hypothesis in mind, you may start asking "leading" questions. This means asking them questions that have expected answers, and this can impact your data because you've "lead" them toward specific answers. Asking, "How do you feel about having a pet?" is a less leading question than, "Why does your pet make you happy?"

Be a good listener: As a follow up to the above tip, it's important to be a very attentive listener while you are interviewing someone. They are dedicating time to your research, and their data is helping you explore your research question, so let them complete their thoughts before prompting them with the next question.

Keep your surveys simple: The best surveys are short and concise. Make sure each question contains just ONE question. For example, asking, "Does your pet make you happy, and why do they make you happy?" is a more complicated question for one to answer, and it's also much more difficult to analyze since the answer contains multiple responses.

Test your data collection tools before you start: If you're running a survey or recording interviews, test out your tools ahead of time. This means filling out the survey yourself to make sure the responses are stored correctly, or recording several minutes of footage and testing the playback. Nothing sucks more than getting ready to collect information only to find that the tools you're using aren't working!

Create a contract. You should always provide some sort of written agreement for your participants. This helps to protect both of you, and to ensure that the participant is OK with you recording them or documenting their responses.

LESSON ACTIVITY

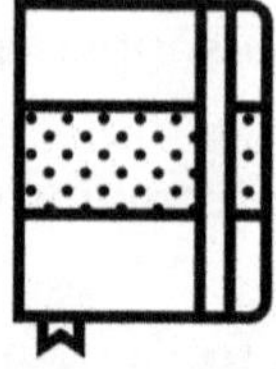

Try recording or documenting a piece of data to help you answer a simple question. What tools did you use to collect this information? Did you run into any challenges as you did so?

CHAPTER 17
THE FINAL COUNTDOWN

There's an overwhelming amount of information on analyzing data, and it takes professional researchers years to figure out what works best for them and the research they conduct. I don't say that to scare you; I just want to manage expectations. So, we're going to do a Research Analysis 101 overview in this chapter.

The good part? Analyzing data is soooo interesting. Once you get a taste for analysis, it's hard not to do it all the time.

TYPES OF ANALYSIS

We've talked extensively about "qualitative" vs. "quantitative" data. The type of data you collect determines how you analyze it.

ANALYZING QUALITATIVE DATA

Qualitative data is often analyzed through **categorical** analysis. This means that you will put your qualitative data points into categories, and then study the categories. Categories help you identify trends, regardless of the type of qualitative information you've collected (a series of photographs, for instance).

You will want to establish your categories before you look at the data you've collected; you may have some additional ideas as you look through it all, but your categories should help answer your research question.

For example, if you're conducting a study on if/how pets make people happy, your categories may consist of the following:

- Type of animal (1)
- Age of animal (2)
- How long the person has had the animal (3)
- Does the subject feel that the pet has made them happier? (4)
- If so, why? (5)

The answer to these questions may help me address my research question. Then, I can look at a quote from one of my interviews:

"I have a cat named Sofie. She is 7 years old and we adopted her when she was 3. She makes my life better because I like having her sleep next to me, and her purring makes me less anxious when I am dealing with my anxiety."

This quote gives me information that I can assign to each category:

- Cat
- 7 years old
- 4 years

- Yes
- Improves mental health

Now, if I've interviewed 10 people, I may start to notice trends when I categorize their responses. Let's say 7 out of 10 of my subjects have a cat younger than 10 years old, and they all answered that their cat makes them happier in some way. This starts to look like a trend to me, so I will include this in my results section, and I will also refer back to my literature review. (Remember what a literature review is? It's when you read and synthesize existing research on your research topic to see what findings already exist.) Referring back to your literature review helps to strengthen your finding, or perhaps your finding is new to that topic, in which case you can say that there is a need to study this further.

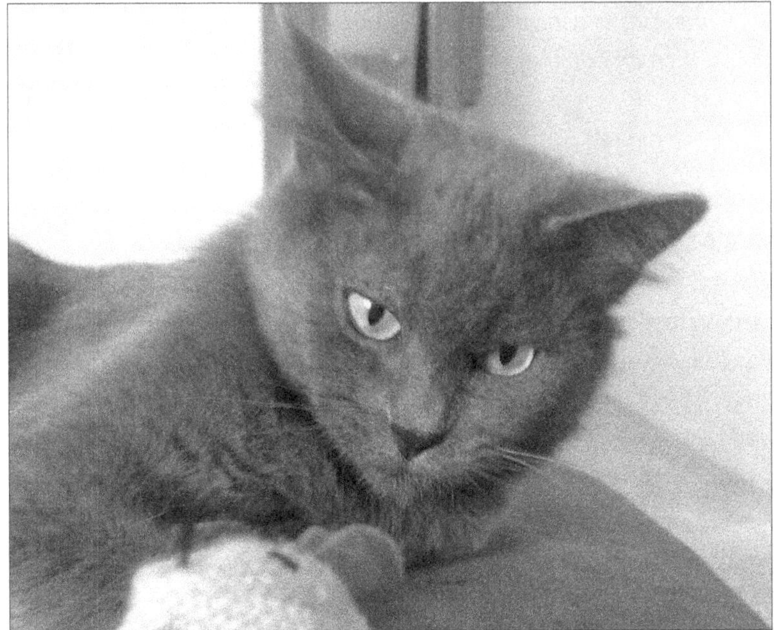

My kitty, Sofie

To bring meaning to the words before you:

- *Identify themes or patterns — ideas, concepts, behaviors, interactions, incidents, terminology or phrases used.*
- *Organize them into coherent categories that summarize and bring meaning to the text.*

This can be fairly labor-intensive depending on the amount of data you have. But this is the crux of qualitative analysis. It involves reading and re-reading the text and identifying coherent categories. You may want to assign abbreviated codes of a few letters, words or symbols and place them next to the themes and ideas you find. This will help organize the data into categories. Provide a descriptive label (name) for each category you create. Be clear about what you include in the category and what you exclude. As you categorize the data, you might identify other themes that serve as subcategories. Continue to categorize until you have identified and labeled all relevant themes.

— University of Wisconsin Cooperative Extension

ANALYZING QUANTITATIVE DATA

Analyzing quantitative data is a whole other ballgame. (Quantitative data refers to numerical data or statistical information, such as survey results or data sets with variables.) Statistical analysis is what's used to analyze quantitative data, and it can quickly seem daunting because it is so technical. Here is a useful guide by the University of Minnesota about the most common types of quantitative analysis:

TYPE OF TEST	USE
CORRELATIONAL	These tests look for an association between variables.
PEARSON CORRELATION	Tests for the strength of the association between two continuous variables.
SPEARMAN CORRELATION	Tests for the strength of the association between two ordinal variables.
CHI-SQUARE	Tests for the strength of the association between two categorical variables.

COMPARISON OF MEANS: LOOK FOR THE DIFFERENCE BETWEEN THE MEANS OF VARIABLES

TYPE OF TEST	USE
PAIRED T-TEST	Tests for the difference between two related variables.
INDEPENDENT T-TEST	Tests for the difference between two independent variables.
ANOVA	Tests the difference between group means after any other variance in the outcome variable is accounted for.

REGRESSION: ASSESS IF CHANGE IN ONE VARIABLE PREDICTS CHANGE IN ANOTHER VARIABLE

TYPE OF TEST	USE
SIMPLE REGRESSION	Tests how change in the predictor variable predicts the level of change in the outcome variable.
MULTIPLE REGRESSION	Tests how change in the combination of two or more predictor variables predict the level of change in the outcome variable.

NON-PARAMETRIC: USED WHEN THE DATA DOES NOT MEET ASSUMPTIONS REQUIRED FOR PARAMETRIC TESTS

TYPE OF TEST	USE
WILCOXON RANK-SUM TEST	Tests for the difference between two independent variables, incl. magnitude/direction of diff.
WILCOXON SIGN-RANK TEST	Tests for the difference between two related variables, incl. magnitude/direction of difference.
SIGN TEST	Tests if two related variables are different — ignores the magnitude of change, only takes into account direction.

It's totally OK if you looked at that and were like, "HUH????"

When people ask me what the most important types of statistical analysis are, I personally think that understanding correlation and a paired T-test is important. Why? Because correlation, particularly, is misrepresented often. Ever heard the phrase, "correlation does not equal causation"? This means that just because there is an association between two variables, this does not mean that the association is CAUSED by either variable. A paired T-test is kind of the opposite of a correlation; it looks for the differences between two variables.

MIXED-METHODS ANALYSIS

You may find that your research topic benefits from a mixed-methods approach. We talked about this a few chapters back; mixed-methods means that you use both qualitative and quantitative data or analysis in your research. (I myself am a mixed-methods researcher, and it's my go-to strategy for most of my studies.)

LESSON ACTIVITY

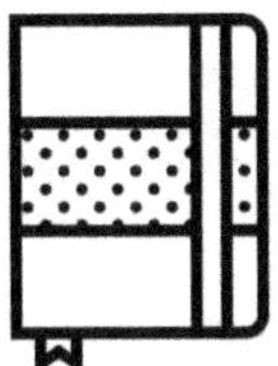

What type of analysis works best for your data? Try to go one step further and determine the categories you want to use for qualitative, or the type of statistical analysis that works best for your quantitative data.

After you've analyzed your data, you'll likely have some results that you're dying to share with the world. In a research article, the results section shares the findings of your study. This is where you'll describe your approach to analysis (how you analyzed your data the way you did) along with what you've found.

One common misconception about results is that you have to "prove" something. That's not what your results are about. The goal of research is to substantiate theories, but one study alone is not enough to constitute proof. This is especially important to remember if your results weren't what you expected, and that's totally OK. It's still helpful for other researchers in that field to know what to continue investigating.

It helps to start your results section with a brief summary of your key findings. These are the most important pieces of information once can take away from your study. From there, you can elaborate on what else you found. Above all, your results should always be directly connected to your research question. Crafting the proper methodology and collection should have prevented collecting too much irrelevant information, but sometimes interesting things arise that were unexpected. However, save that for a future study, and focus your results on what can address your question.

Your results section will likely include some visual representation of your results, such as charts, graphs, tables, or multimedia. No matter what type of data you collected (qualitative or quantitative), visualization helps communicate your results.

Essentially, your results are what you've *found*. Interpreting and synthesizing these results comes after.

What to include in a results section:

- *An Introductory context for understanding the results by restating the research problem underpinning your study. This is useful in orientating the reader's focus back to the research after reading about the methods of data gathering and analysis.*
- *Inclusion of non-textual elements, such as, figures, charts, photos, maps, tables, etc. to further illustrate key findings, if appropriate. Rather than relying entirely on descriptive text, consider the ways your findings can be presented visually. This is a helpful way of condensing a lot of data into one place that can then be referred to in the text. Consider using appendices if there is a lot of non-textual elements.*
- *A systematic description of your results, highlighting for the reader observations that are most relevant to the topic under investigation [remember that not all results that emerge from the methodology used to gather information may be related to answering the "So What?" question]. Do not confuse observations with interpretations; observations in this context refers to highlighting important findings you discovered through a process of reviewing prior literature and gathering data.*
- *The page length of your results section is guided by the amount and types of data to be reported. However, focus*

only on findings that are important and related to addressing the research problem. It is not uncommon to have unanticipated results that are not relevant to answering the research question, and this is not to say that you don't acknowledge tangential findings, but spending time describing them only clutters your overall results section.

- *A short paragraph that concludes the results section by synthesizing the key findings of the study. Highlight the most important findings you want readers to remember as they transition into the discussion section. This is particularly important if, for example, there are many results to report, the findings are complicated or unanticipated, or they are impactful or actionable in some way [i.e., able to be acted upon in a feasible way applied to practice].*

— from the University of Southern California Library

VISUALIZING YOUR DATA

Have you looked at a map lately? Or a chart? Chances are, you've encountered some type of data visualization in your day-to-day life. Understanding types of visualizations may help you figure out which one may work best for your data. Here are some common types of visualizations:

- 1D/linear: This refers to a list of data points.
- 2D/planar: It's easiest to think of these as "maps," as they usually (but not always) visualize geospatial data.
- 3D/volumetric: 3D models or visualizations that have a volume-based metric (just like it sounds!).
- Temporal: Lots of visualizations fall into this category, but you're likely familiar with a timeline or a histogram.
- nD/Multidimensional: This may sound fancy, but many of these are ones you see frequently, such as a pie chart.
- Tree/hierarchal: Think of a family tree, for example.

LESSON ACTIVITY

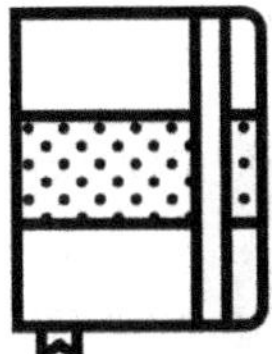

What type of data visualization would be the most effective to convey your results? As you're looking at your results, are there any that don't respond to your research question in some way? If so, why do you think that happened?

INTERVIEW WITH A RESEARCHER

NAME:
Elise Gornish
ROLE:
Cooperative Extension Specialist in Ecological Restoration
AFFILIATION:
University of Arizona

How is research a part of your job?

A big part of my job is to help managers figure out how to best design and deploy approaches for ecological restoration and invasive plant control on natural and working landscapes. I conduct research to identify best strategies. For example, I am currently investigating how functional overlap of plant traits might provide utility for weed management.

What is your educational and professional background?

I have a PhD in Ecology and spent two years as a postdoc, which is a pretty typical route to my position.

What are your favorite research tools?

I love field work and so do the people in my lab. We collect tons of data related to plant communities and often use statistical approaches that can accommodate these big data sets, including community ordination, and structural equation modeling.

What type of research do you conduct?

We largely investigate how individual plants, plant populations and plant communities respond to management as well as look at how plants can be used to restore multiple ecosystem services. Right now, we are particularly interested in how particular plant traits might confer utility for achieving multiple management goals (forage production, weed control, erosion control, and native species reestablishment) on arid landscapes.

How do you evaluate the impact of your research?

In academia, most people can evaluate the impact of their research by following citation rate of peer-reviewed publications. This is useful, however, lots of the folks that need and use our research are not in academia and therefore, do not read peer-reviewed literature. We deliver science to these stakeholders through outreach and extension programs such as workshops, field days, blog posts and white papers. Measuring the impact of our work through these avenues can be accomplished through formal written surveys, semi-structured interviews and informal discussions with clientele.

We deliver science to these stakeholders through outreach and extension programs such as workshops, field days, blog posts, and white papers.

Can you share some insight into the process of publishing research?

Publishing is important and necessary in academia. Publication rate is effectively academic currency. It is a sometimes difficult process that can be fraught with politics and other obnoxious factors not at all associated with the core science. However, your science can only contribute to the development of new ideas and policies if other researchers are aware of your work, which necessitates publication. Generally, we publish in applied journals as our work is most relevant to readers of those journals. We also spend considerable effort to publish overviews of our work in non peer-reviewed publications in order to extend the delivery of our science to non-academics. This means that we publicize our work in various social media postings, and produce white papers and opinion pieces in special interest journals.

Publishing is important and necessary in academia. Publication rate is effectively academic currency.

How can a citizen researcher learn more about science?

There are tons of outlets from which to learn about science. Some are obvious and highly relevant (e.g. science section of the New York Times, National Geographic Magazine, etc.), but many are less obvious and are more targeted (i.e. botanical gardens, Twitter, outreach blogs). A google search of 'science news' will bring up literally thousands of sites that provide overviews of current research efforts covering a variety of fields. Something else to keep in mind is that most academic or research outlets will have information directed at non scientists. For example, NASA and NOAA both make considerable effort to provide outreach and education materials on their websites. Many university researchers are also understanding the value of outreach and will provide research briefs on their websites.

Science is integral for the development of ideas and technologies that improve all aspects of daily life for living things. Science should be respected and celebrated by researchers and non-researchers alike, and this means supporting the cultivation and funding of science at all levels of government. Citizens can show support for science by making clear to their elected representatives just how important they think science teaching, support, and funding is.

> *Science is integral for the development of ideas and technologies that improve all aspects of daily life for living things.*

ELISE IN ACTION:

CHAPTER 19
A CITE TO SEE

When a researcher has finished writing and compiling their research paper — complete with a literature review, methodology, results, discussion, and citation sections — the next step is often to get it published. Publishing research helps expose it to others in that given field, which means that other researchers can continue building on that topic. (In Part 1, we talked a bit about publishing in traditional academic journals, as well as a newer approach of open access.)

Getting published in an academic journal can be tricky. There's much value in academic journals, but the process is often long, and can be frustrating to researchers who want to get their findings out into the world as soon as possible. The process usually resembles something like this:

- A researcher will prepare the paper with collaborating researchers.
- They will submit it to a journal, sometimes with a submission fee (this is intended to go toward peer review costs).
- Peer reviewers will read and critique the paper, looking closely at the methodology to ensure that the science was conducted correctly.

126

- After the peer reviewers are finished, they will accept the paper, reject it, or recommend updates to the researchers. If rejected, a researcher can revise the paper and try submitting it to another publication.

MEASURING RESEARCH IMPACT

Professional researchers must measure the impact of their research; essentially, this means measuring how their findings have impacted their field or topic. This serves a few purposes. It helps researchers justify their research topic/approach if they can demonstrate that it's had an impact on the world in some way. These measurements also help determine funding or support from institutions. This is not to say that all research must have a measurable impact for it to be deemed "worthy" or "important," but it can help to clarify direction and interest.

Researchers measure this in a few ways. One of the main ways is through citations. If a researcher is being cited often by others in their field, this increases their impact. The measurement system of this varies within fields and industries. This is referred to as an "h-index": "an author-level metric that attempts to measure both the productivity and citation impact of the publications of a scientist or scholar. The index is based on the set of the scientist's most cited papers and the number of citations that they have received in other publications." (via Wikipedia)

A "g-index" works similarly. It measures research productivity based on how many times an author has been published. So it helps to think of h-index as a **citation-based** metric, and g-index as a **publication-based** metric.

This table from NC State University outlines some of the parameters of these metrics:

	h-index	**g-index**
ATTEMPTS TO MEASURE:	Quality and quantity of author's work	Quality and quantitative of author's work, with more weight on quality
CALCULATION:	An author's h-index is the number of papers (h) that have received (h) or more citations. An author with an h-index of 8 has 8 papers cited at least 8 times.	To calculate the g-index an author's articles are ranked in decreasing order of the number of the citations each received. The unique largest number such that the top g articles received, together, at least g^2 citations is the g-index.
LIMITATIONS:	• Inaccurate measure of early career research impact. • Only measures published works.	Only measures published works.

LESSON ACTIVITY

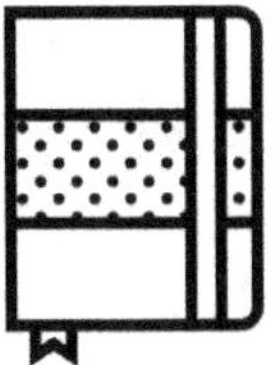

Try going back to the activity from Chapter 1, where you were tasked with finding an article in a journal, and apply everything you've learned about the research process.

Do you feel like you have a better understanding of how research is conducted?

What aspects of research are you still curious about?

CHAPTER 20
THE CITIZEN RESEARCHER MANIFESTO

Congratulations, dear reader — you're well on your way to making research a more important part of your life. Now that you know the basics of research, what happens next?

It is my hope that you come away with a greater appreciation for research, science, and data in your day to day life. Have you noticed how much it makes a difference in our lives? We live in an amazing time, where nearly all research is available to us at our finger tips.

This book just barely scratches the surface of what research and science entails. As such, I hope you'll be inspired to continue your journey.

Ultimately, my goal is to help make research more accessible and exciting for all, and now you're equipped to aid in that quest.

This is the **Citizen Researcher Manifesto**, and I hope you'll join me in following this creed:

I commit to being a more conscientious reader and critic of the information I consume;

I commit to supporting public access to research, data, and science;

I commit to facilitating peer review in my day-to-day life, holding my friends and family accountable for the information we consume and share;

I commit to conducting my own citizen research ethically and transparently;

Above all, I commit to wielding research, data, and science for good.

RECOMMENDATIONS

Here are books, podcasts, and resources I recommend to all citizen researchers. Enjoy creating your research library!

. . . .

The Information: A History, A Theory, A Flood by James Gleick
A fascinating book about the history of information, language, and communication.

A Very Short, Fairly Interesting and Reasonably Cheap Book about Qualitative Research by David Silverman
A fast, funny and useful read about how to do qualitative research.

Oh No Ross and Carrie
An entertaining podcast for skeptics, in which hosts Ross Blocher and Carrie Poppy delve into science, spirituality, and claims of the paranormal. A great example of how to be a citizen researcher.

Gastropod
Gastropod is a podcast (what can I say, I love podcasts!) about food—the science, research, and culture of it. Co-hosts Cynthia Graber and Nicole Twilley interview scientists and specialists for expertise and insight on all sorts of unique food topics (like kombucha!).

BrainPickings.com
Brain Pickings is an online publication created by Maria Popova who calls it "an inventory of cross-disciplinary interestingness." Many of the articles are about the beauty, impact, and sometimes sheer wackiness of science.

The Demon-Haunted World: Science as a Candle in the Dark by Carl Sagan
A classic Sagan book that explores the beauty of science and the importance of scientific thinking as we progress into the future.

LIBRARY CLASSIFICATION

Dewey Decimal System

Class 000 – Computer science, information & general works
Class 100 – Philosophy & psychology
Class 200 – Religion
Class 300 – Social sciences
Class 400 – Language
Class 500 – Science
Class 600 – Technology
Class 700 – Arts & recreation
Class 800 – Literature
Class 900 – History & geography

. . . .

Library of Congress

Class A – General Works
Class B – Philosophy, Psychology, Religion
Class C – Auxiliary Sciences of History (General)
Class D – World History (except American History)
Class E – American History
Class F – Local History of the United States and British,
Dutch, French, and Latin America
Class G – Geography, Anthropology, Recreation
Class H – Social Sciences
Class J – Political Science
Class K – Law
Class L – Education
Class M – Music
Class N – Fine Arts

Class P – Language and Literature
Class Q – Science
Class R – Medicine
Class S – Agriculture
Class T – Technology
Class U – Military Science
Class V – Naval Science
Class Z – Bibliography, Library Science

GLOSSARY OF RESEARCH TERMS

Accuracy — a term used in survey research to refer to the match between the target population and the sample.

Affective Measures — procedures or devices used to obtain quantified descriptions of an individual's feelings, emotional states, or dispositions.

Aggregate — a total created from smaller units. For instance, the population of a county is an aggregate of the populations of the cities, rural areas, etc. that comprise the county. As a verb, it refers to total data from smaller units into a large unit.

Anonymity — a research condition in which no one, including the researcher, knows the identities of research participants.

Baseline — a control measurement carried out before an experimental treatment.

Behaviorism — school of psychological thought concerned with the observable, tangible, objective facts of behavior, rather than with subjective phenomena such as thoughts, emotions, or impulses. Contemporary behaviorism also emphasizes the study of mental states such as feelings and fantasies to the extent that they can be directly observed and measured.

Beliefs — ideas, doctrines, tenets, etc. that are accepted as true on grounds which are not immediately susceptible to rigorous proof.

Benchmarking — systematically measuring and comparing the operations and outcomes of organizations, systems, processes, etc., against agreed upon "best-in-class" frames of reference.

Bias — a loss of balance and accuracy in the use of research methods. It can appear in research via the sampling frame, random sampling, or non-response. It can also occur at other stages in research, such as while interviewing, in the design of questions, or in the way data are analyzed and presented. Bias means that the research findings will not be representative of, or generalizable to, a wider population.

Case Study — the collection and presentation of detailed information about a particular participant or small group, frequently including data derived from the subjects themselves.

Causal Hypothesis — a statement hypothesizing that the independent variable affects the dependent variable in some way.

Causal Relationship — the relationship established that shows that an independent variable, and nothing else, causes a change in a dependent variable. It also establishes how much of a change is shown in the dependent variable.

Causality — the relation between cause and effect.

Central Tendency — any way of describing or characterizing typical, average, or common values in some distribution.

Chi-square Analysis — a common non-parametric statistical test which compares an expected proportion or ratio to an actual proportion or ratio.

Claim — a statement, similar to a hypothesis, which is made in response to the research question and that is affirmed with evidence based on research.

Classification — ordering of related phenomena into categories, groups, or systems according to characteristics or attributes.

Cluster Analysis — a method of statistical analysis where data that share a common trait are grouped together. The data is collected in a way that allows the data collector to group data according to certain characteristics.

Cohort Analysis — group by group analytic treatment of individuals having a statistical factor in common to each group. Group members share a particular characteristic [e.g., born in a given year] or a common experience [e.g., entering a college at a given time].

Confidentiality — a research condition in which no one except the researcher(s) knows the identities of the participants in a study. It refers to the treatment of information that a participant has disclosed to the researcher in a relationship of trust and with the expectation that it will not be revealed to others in ways that violate the original consent agreement, unless permission is granted by the participant.

Confirmability Objectivity — the findings of the study could be confirmed by another person conducting the same study.

Construct — refers to any of the following: something that exists theoretically but is not directly observable; a concept developed [constructed] for describing relations among phenomena or for other research purposes; or, a theoretical definition in which concepts are defined in terms of other concepts.

Construct Validity — seeks an agreement between a theoretical concept and a specific measuring device, such as observation.

Constructivism — the idea that reality is socially constructed. It is the view that reality cannot be understood outside of the way humans interact and that the idea that knowledge is constructed, not discovered. Constructivists believe that learning is more active and self-directed than either behaviorism or cognitive theory would postulate.

Content Analysis — the systematic, objective, and quantitative description of the manifest or latent content of print or nonprint communications.

Context Sensitivity — awareness by a qualitative researcher of factors such as values and beliefs that influence cultural behaviors.

Control Group — the group in an experimental design that receives either no treatment or a different treatment from the experimental group. This group can thus be compared to the experimental group.

Controlled Experiment — an experimental design with two or more randomly selected groups [an experimental group and control group] in which the researcher controls or introduces the independent variable and measures the dependent variable at least two times [pre- and post-test measurements].

Correlation — a common statistical analysis, usually abbreviated as r, that measures the degree of relationship between pairs of interval variables in a sample. The range of correlation is from -1.00 to zero to +1.00. Also, a non-cause and effect relationship between two variables.

Covariate — a product of the correlation of two related variables times their standard deviations. Used in true experiments to measure the difference of treatment between them.

Credibility — a researcher's ability to demonstrate that the object of a study is accurately identified and described based on the way in which the study was conducted.

Critical Theory — an evaluative approach to social science research, associated with Germany's neo-Marxist "Frankfurt School," that aims to criticize as well as analyze society, opposing the political orthodoxy of modern communism. Its goal is to promote human emancipatory forces and to expose ideas and systems that impede them.

Data — factual information [as measurements or statistics] used as a basis for reasoning, discussion, or calculation.

Data Mining — the process of analyzing data from different perspectives and summarizing it into useful information, often to discover patterns and/or systematic relationships among variables.

Data Quality — this is the degree to which the collected data [results of measurement or observation] meet the standards of quality to be considered valid [trustworthy] and reliable [dependable].

Deductive — a form of reasoning in which conclusions are formulated about particulars from general or universal premises.

Dependability — being able to account for changes in the design of the study and the changing conditions surrounding what was studied.

Dependent Variable — a variable that varies due, at least in part, to the impact of the independent variable. In other words, its value "depends" on the value of the independent variable. For example, in the variables "gender" and "academic major," academic major is the dependent variable, meaning that your major cannot determine whether you are male or female, but your gender might indirectly lead you to favor one major over another.

Deviation — the distance between the mean and a particular data point in a given distribution.

Discourse Community — a community of scholars and researchers in a given field who respond to and communicate to each other through published articles in the community's journals and presentations at conventions. All members of the discourse community adhere to certain conventions for the presentation of their theories and research.

Discrete Variable — a variable that is measured solely in whole units, such as, gender and number of siblings.

Distribution — the range of values of a particular variable.

Effect Size — the amount of change in a dependent variable that can be attributed to manipulations of the independent variable. A large effect size exists when the value of the dependent variable is strongly influenced by the independent variable. It is the mean difference on a variable between experimental and control groups divided by the standard deviation on that variable of the pooled groups or of the control group alone.

Emancipatory Research — research is conducted on and with people from marginalized groups or communities. It is led by a researcher or research team who is either an indigenous or external insider; is interpreted within intellectual frameworks of that group; and, is conducted largely for the purpose of empowering members of that community and improving services for them. It also engages members of the community as co-constructors or validators of knowledge.

Empirical Research — the process of developing systematized knowledge gained from observations that are formulated to support insights and generalizations about the phenomena being researched.

Epistemology — concerns knowledge construction; asks what constitutes knowledge and how knowledge is validated.

Ethnography — method to study groups and/or cultures over a period of time. The goal of this type of research is to comprehend the particular group/culture through immersion into the culture or group. Research is completed through various methods but, since the researcher is immersed within the group for an extended period of time, more detailed information is usually collected during the research.

Expectancy Effect — any unconscious or conscious cues that convey to the participant in a study how the researcher wants them to respond. Expecting someone to behave in a particular way has been shown to promote the expected behavior. Expectancy effects can be minimized by using standardized interactions with subjects, automated data-gathering methods, and double blind protocols.

External Validity — the extent to which the results of a study are generalizable or transferable.

Factor Analysis — a statistical test that explores relationships among data. The test explores which variables in a data set are most related to each other. In a carefully constructed survey, for example, factor analysis can yield information on patterns of responses, not simply data on a single response. Larger tendencies may then be interpreted, indicating behavior trends rather than simply responses to specific questions.

Field Studies — academic or other investigative studies undertaken in a natural setting, rather than in laboratories, classrooms, or other structured environments.

Focus Groups — small, roundtable discussion groups charged with examining specific topics or problems, including possible options or solutions. Focus groups usually consist of 4-12 participants, guided by moderators to keep the discussion flowing and to collect and report the results.

Framework — the structure and support that may be used as both the launching point and the on-going guidelines for investigating a research problem.

Generalizability — the extent to which research findings and conclusions conducted on a specific study to groups or situations can be applied to the population at large.

Grounded Theory — practice of developing other theories that emerge from observing a group. Theories are grounded in the group's observable experiences, but researchers add their own insight into why those experiences exist.

Group Behavior — behaviors of a group as a whole, as well as the behavior of an individual as influenced by his or her membership in a group.

Hypothesis — a tentative explanation based on theory to predict a causal relationship between variables.

Independent Variable — the conditions of an experiment that are systematically manipulated by the researcher. A variable that is not impacted by the dependent variable, and that itself impacts the dependent variable. In the earlier example of "gender" and "academic major," (see Dependent Variable) gender is the independent variable.

Individualism — a theory or policy having primary regard for the liberty, rights, or independent actions of individuals.

Inductive — a form of reasoning in which a generalized conclusion is formulated from particular instances.

Inductive Analysis — a form of analysis based on inductive reasoning; a researcher using inductive analysis starts with answers, but formulates questions throughout the research process.

Insiderness — a concept in qualitative research that refers to the degree to which a researcher has access to and an understanding of persons, places, or things within a group or community based on being a member of that group or community.

Internal Consistency — the extent to which all questions or items assess the same characteristic, skill, or quality.

Internal Validity — the rigor with which the study was conducted [e.g., the study's design, the care taken to conduct measurements, and decisions concerning what was and was not measured]. It is also the extent to which the designers of a study have taken into account alternative explanations for any causal relationships they explore. In studies that do not explore causal relationships, only the first of these definitions should be considered when assessing internal validity.

Margin of Error — the permittable or acceptable deviation from the target or a specific value. The allowance for slight error or miscalculation or changing circumstances in a study. Measurement -- process of obtaining a numerical description of the extent to which persons, organizations, or things possess specified characteristics.

Meta-Analysis — an analysis combining the results of several studies that address a set of related hypotheses.

Methodology — a theory or analysis of how research does and should proceed.

Methods — systematic approaches to the conduct of an operation or process. It includes steps of procedure, application of techniques, systems of reasoning or analysis, and the modes of inquiry employed by a discipline.

Mixed-Methods — a research approach that uses two or more methods from both the quantitative and qualitative research categories. It is also referred to as blended methods, combined methods, or methodological triangulation.

Modeling — the creation of a physical or computer analogy to understand a particular phenomenon. Modeling helps in estimating the relative magnitude of various factors involved in a phenomenon. A successful model can be shown to account for unexpected behavior that has been observed, to predict certain behaviors, which can then be tested experimentally, and to demonstrate that a given theory cannot account for certain phenomenon.

Models — representations of objects, principles, processes, or ideas often used for imitation or emulation.

Norm — the norm in statistics is the average or usual performance. For example, students usually complete their high school graduation requirements when they are 18 years old. Even though some students graduate when they are younger or older, the norm is that any given student will graduate when he or she is 18 years old.

Null Hypothesis — the proposition, to be tested statistically, that the experimental intervention has "no effect," meaning that the treatment and control groups will not differ as a result of the intervention. Investigators usually hope that the data will demonstrate some effect from the intervention, thus allowing the investigator to reject the null hypothesis.

Ontology — a discipline of philosophy that explores the science of what is, the kinds and structures of objects, properties, events, processes, and relations in every area of reality.

Panel Study — a longitudinal study in which a group of individuals is interviewed at intervals over a period of time.

Participant — individuals whose physiological and/or behavioral characteristics and responses are the object of study in a research project.

Peer-Review — the process in which the author of a book, article, or other type of publication submits his or her work to experts in the field for critical evaluation, usually prior to publication. This is standard procedure in publishing scholarly research.

Phenomenology — a qualitative research approach concerned with understanding certain group behaviors from that group's point of view.

Philosophy — critical examination of the grounds for fundamental beliefs and analysis of the basic concepts, doctrines, or practices that express such beliefs.

Policy — governing principles that serve as guidelines or rules for decision making and action in a given area.

Policy Analysis — systematic study of the nature, rationale, cost, impact, effectiveness, implications, etc., of existing or alternative policies, using the theories and methodologies of relevant social science disciplines.

Population — the target group under investigation. The population is the entire set under consideration. Samples are drawn from populations.

Positivism — a doctrine in the philosophy of science, positivism argues that science can only deal with observable entities known directly to experience. The positivist aims to construct general laws, or theories, which express relationships between phenomena. Observation and experiment is used to show whether the phenomena fit the theory.

Predictive Measurement — use of tests, inventories, or other measures to determine or estimate future events, conditions, outcomes, or trends.

Principal Investigator — the scientist or scholar with primary responsibility for the design and conduct of a research project.

Probability — the chance that a phenomenon will occur randomly. As a statistical measure, it is shown as p [the "p" factor].

Qualitative — is a method of inquiry employed in many different academic disciplines, including in the social sciences and natural sciences but also in non-academic contexts including market research, business, and service demonstrations by non-profits.

Quantitative — emphasize objective measurements and the statistical, mathematical, or numerical analysis of data collected through polls, questionnaires, and surveys, or by manipulating pre-existing statistical data using computational techniques.

Questionnaire — structured sets of questions on specified subjects that are used to gather information, attitudes, or opinions.

Random Sampling — a process used in research to draw a sample of a population strictly by chance, yielding no discernible pattern beyond chance. Random sampling can be accomplished by first numbering the population, then selecting the sample according to a table of random numbers or using a random-number computer generator. The sample is said to be random because there is no regular or discernible pattern or order. Random sample selection is used under the assumption that sufficiently large samples assigned randomly will exhibit a distribution comparable to that of the population from which the sample is drawn. The random assignment of participants increases the probability that differences observed between participant groups are the result of the experimental intervention.

Reliability — the degree to which a measure yields consistent results. If the measuring instrument [e.g., survey] is reliable, then administering it to similar groups would yield similar results. Reliability is a prerequisite for validity. An unreliable indicator cannot produce trustworthy results.

Representative Sample — sample in which the participants closely match the characteristics of the population, and thus, all segments of the population are represented in the sample. A representative sample allows results to be generalized from the sample to the population.

Rigor — degree to which research methods are scrupulously and meticulously carried out in order to recognize important influences occurring in an experimental study.

Sample — the population researched in a particular study. Usually, attempts are made to select a "sample population" that is considered representative of groups of people to whom results will be generalized or transferred. In studies that use inferential statistics to analyze results or which are designed to be generalizable, sample size is critical, generally the larger the number in the sample, the higher the likelihood of a representative distribution of the population.

Sampling Error — the degree to which the results from the sample deviate from those that would be obtained from the entire population, because of random error in the selection of respondent and the corresponding reduction in reliability.

Saturation — a situation in which data analysis begins to reveal repetition and redundancy and when new data tend to confirm existing findings rather than expand upon them.

Semantics — the relationship between symbols and meaning in a linguistic system. Also, the cuing system that connects what is written in the text to what is stored in the reader's prior knowledge.

Standard Deviation — a measure of variation that indicates the typical distance between the scores of a distribution and the mean; it is determined by taking the square root of the average of the squared deviations in a given distribution. It can be used to indicate the proportion of data within certain ranges of scale values when the distribution conforms closely to the normal curve.

Statistical Analysis — application of statistical processes and theory to the compilation, presentation, discussion, and interpretation of numerical data.

Statistical Bias — characteristics of an experimental or sampling design, or the mathematical treatment of data, that systematically affects the results of a study so as to produce incorrect, unjustified, or inappropriate inferences or conclusions.

Statistical Significance — the probability that the difference between the outcomes of the control and experimental group are great enough that it is unlikely due solely to chance. The probability that the null hypothesis can be rejected at a predetermined significance level [0.05 or 0.01].

Statistical Tests — researchers use statistical tests to make quantitative decisions about whether a study's data indicate a significant effect from the intervention and allow the researcher to reject the null hypothesis. That is, statistical tests show whether the differences between the outcomes of the control and experimental groups are great enough to be statistically significant. If differences are found to be statistically significant, it means that the probability [likelihood] that these differences occurred solely due to chance is relatively low. Most researchers agree that a significance value of .05 or less [i.e., there is a 95% probability that the differences are real] sufficiently determines significance.

Subcultures — ethnic, regional, economic, or social groups exhibiting characteristic patterns of behavior sufficient to distinguish them from the larger society to which they belong.

Testing — the act of gathering and processing information about individuals' ability, skill, understanding, or knowledge under controlled conditions.

Theory — a general explanation about a specific behavior or set of events that is based on known principles and serves to organize related events in a meaningful way. A theory is not as specific as a hypothesis.

Trend Samples — method of sampling different groups of

people at different points in time from the same population.

Triangulation — a multi-method or pluralistic approach, using different methods in order to focus on the research topic from different viewpoints and to produce a multi-faceted set of data. Also used to check the validity of findings from any one method.

Unit of Analysis — the basic observable entity or phenomenon being analyzed by a study and for which data are collected in the form of variables.

Validity — the degree to which a study accurately reflects or assesses the specific concept that the researcher is attempting to measure. A method can be reliable, consistently measuring the same thing, but not valid.

Variable — any characteristic or trait that can vary from one person to another [race, gender, academic major] or for one person over time [age, political beliefs].

Weighted Scores — scores in which the components are modified by different multipliers to reflect their relative importance.

Definitions sourced from the Free Social Science Dictionary.

ACKNOWLEDGEMENTS

I'm grateful to everyone who helped bring this book to life! Big thanks to my husband, who has mostly seen my face obscured by my laptop for the past several months; and my mom, who champions for me tirelessly. (The Beyoncé meme was just for you.) And a hearty belly scratch to my kitty, Sofie, who is the most excellent writing buddy.

Thank you to Dana Witwicki who connected me with 500 Women Scientists (www.500womenscientists.org) for the research interviews in this book. The work you all do is so inspiring. Shout-out to the MBMBaMBrarians Facebook group for the additional support and insight.

And, last but not least, thank you to everyone who signed up for the original email series, including my cousin Shauna, who has been a wonderful supporter of this project from the get-go.

ABOUT THE AUTHOR

Ashley Warren is a researcher and award-winning journalist based in Reno, Nevada. She is the founder of Ashley Warren Research, which provides research expertise to people around the world. She holds a Master's degree in Literacy Studies, with an emphasis on research and library science, from the University of Nevada, Reno. Ashley is a member of the American Library Association, the National Council for Teachers of English, and the Association of Professional Genealogists.

WWW.ASHLEYWARRENRESEARCH.COM

www.ingramcontent.com/pod-product-compliance
Lightning Source LLC
Chambersburg PA
CBHW061932270726
48660CB00004BA/1515